How To Have A Good Marriage

How To Have A Good Marriage

Before and After the Wedding

Dr. Mark W. Lee

CHRISTIAN HERALD BOOKS
Chappaqua, New York

Library of Congress Cataloging in Publication Data
Lee, Mark W. 1923—
    How to Have a Good Marriage

    1. Marriage. I. Title.
BV835.L44   301.42   78-56974
ISBN 0-915684-39-X

FIRST EDITION

CHRISTIAN HERALD BOOKS,
40 OVERLOOK DRIVE, CHAPPAQUA, NEW YORK 10514

PERMISSIONS: We acknowledge with appreciation permission to re-
print brief passages from:
The Adventure of Living, by Paul Tournier. Harper and Row, 1965.
The Los Angeles Times, July 10, 1977.

To the students in my life,
especially to those
who shared
their dreams, hopes, expectations
and questions in preparation
for marriage and
the family

Table of Contents

Preface

When does a good marriage begin? Some couples report that the unhappiest experiences in their relationship occurred during the engagement period. They say that dating before their commitment to marriage was a happy time, and marriage with all its pressures was at least a trade-off from one set of problems and frustrations to another. But the engagement became, for many, a transition period when differences weighed heavily on the prospective bride and groom. Arguments, even petty jealousies, blocked communication. At the time some counselees felt, "If we argue *now*, what will marriage be like?" They felt that marriage would become what the engagement period was, only more so.

If the engagement period is taken seriously and used for careful marriage preparation, future experience becomes more promising. Investing time to investigate all relevant matters, seeking premarital counseling, and following through on a rigorous preparation program, persons may expect to be successful in their marriages. My own records show highly favorable marriage statistics for those couples who completed premarital testing and counseling. About one-third of the engaged couples who launched the preparatory program dropped out of the sessions. Some of these married nonetheless. For them, separation and divorce was not an uncommon eventuality.

The largest impediment to premarital counseling is that it is sought after the engagement has been announced. After the plans have been finalized counseling is requested. Some of the counseling sessions reveal that many of these potential marriages should be called off. A few are, but couples should begin premarital counseling soon after their agreement to enter an engagement period, and before their commitments are public knowledge.

Some couples ask for premarital counseling to discover if they *ought to become engaged*. Such counseling is possible, but it is technically not "premarital." It is *pre-engagement* and includes different questions. In premarital counseling, some issues are added, some omitted. Very little pre-engagement counseling is done, and it is not easy to do. Perhaps couples should take college courses in marriage and the family before they consider becoming engaged. The approach will be more objective, less intimate, than premarital counseling. Counseling a specific couple before engagement is a deeply personal matter. It should take place as soon as the couple first seriously considers engagement and continue through two or three sessions.

Agreements between a man and woman made before marriage seem to be taken far more seriously than agreements after marriage. Perhaps this is because they are voluntary and self-giving. After marriage mates often feel they *must* do this or that. Their actions appear to be compelled by events rather than chosen by free assent. Today compulsion is felt to be ugly and unfair.

This book deals with both premarital and postmarital questions. The first of its two sections is short and relates primarily to singles. It assumes that the unmarried life can be appropriate, fulfilling and attractive and that it may be God's will for many persons. God provides us with *options* as to marital status, the single life and the married life, either of which is legitimate and God-given. If a person chooses to remain unmarried, more detailed information about his preparation for mature living will be found in other books.

The second section is for those who opt for the married life. In it I give answers to fifty questions I have used in extensive experience as a premarital counselor.

The book can be used by ministers and counselors who are preparing couples for marriage or counseling couples with marital problems, but couples may choose to help themselves by working through the questions on their own. Many married couples have used these questions to give a new dimension to their marriages and have improved them dramatically.

Every author owes appreciation and acknowledgement to those who assist him in his work, but a few words at the beginning of a book seem insufficient for the purpose. My largest debt is to my secretary, Yvonne Cederblom, who has typed miles of lines; my wife, Fern, who read and offered her critique of the manuscript; my trustees at Simpson College, who encourage me in my work; and my counselees, who provide case studies, ideas, problems and solutions. Without their support and services, my goals could not have been accomplished.

To Be
Or Not
To Be Two

CHAPTER ONE

Confusion About Singles

> *Now, to deal with the matters you wrote about. A*
> *man does well not to marry. But because there is so*
> *much immorality, every man should have his own*
> *wife, and every woman should have her own*
> *husband. . . . Actually I would prefer that all of*
> *you were as I am; but each one has a special gift of*
> *God, one person this gift, another one that gift.*
> *Now, to the unmarried and to the widows I say*
> *that it would be better for you to continue to live*
> *alone as I do.   (1 Corinthians 7:1-2, 7-8 GNB)*

The single Christian should be aware that many eminent persons in the history of the church have been single. Jesus, himself single, also appears to have had many unmarried friends. Mary, Martha, Lazarus, perhaps Mary Magdelene, appear to have been single. Among the disciples only Peter is referred to in the Gospels as married. The Apostle Paul does refer to married apostles in I Corinthians 9. The marital status of a person does not seem to have been a concern of the New Testament writers unless it is an intrinsic part of the violation of some moral principle. John the Baptist lost his head for his criticism of an incestuous marriage (Matthew 14:3-12). Jesus told a startled Samaritan woman that she had a succession of husbands during her lifetime, and the man with whom she was living did not qualify as a husband (John 4:5-29). Paul was incensed at a marriage in Corinth in which a man had married a woman who appears to have been his stepmother—a woman who may have left the father for the

15

son (I Corinthians 5:1-5). The writers of the New Testament do not refer to their own families nor provide specifics from marriages like that of Aquila and Priscilla.

Most of the saints, men and women of the Catholic church whom we remember, were unmarried. Some, like Augustine, had led dissolute and sensuous lives before their conversions but afterward practiced celibacy. Most, like Francis of Assisi, appear to have been idealists and sexually innocent. Their personal devotion to God was partly expressed in their celibacy. They accented the words of I Corinthians 7:32-33—"He that is unmarried careth for the things that belong to the Lord, how he may please the Lord: But he that is married careth for the things that are of the world, how he may please his wife." The Apostle Paul continues in the following verse to counsel single or virgin women as he has just counseled single men. This is unusual procedure— to address men specifically and then to address women with repetition of virtually everything except the gender of the subject. When addressing men and women in other situations, biblical counsel generally varies, the duties of the sexes are differentiated, or the application of the passage to both sexes is implied. But in this case, after referring to his own preference for men and women to remain unmarried, the Apostle Paul summarizes the spiritual reason for doing so: ". . . that ye may attend upon the Lord without distraction." Even so, the Apostle leaves no doubt that to be single or married is not a matter of sin. Whether persons are single or married, they "do well," he says. And the choice of either marriage or no marriage is left to the individual without either status being honored above the other.

In modern times eminent Protestant Christians have been single and served effectively in various ministries. Clarence Macartney, a bachelor, served for several decades as the eminent pastor of First Presbyterian Church in Pittsburgh, Pennsylvania. Miss Henrietta Mears was referred to during her productive years as the most influential Christian woman and church education leader in the western

United States. Fanny Crosby and Amy Carmichael, both hymn writers, were unmarried. Corrie ten Boom never married, although she considered marriage seriously on one occasion in her youth. John Stott, international speaker, biblical student and writer, devoted his life exclusively to the Christian ministry. Other Christian leaders, like C. S. Lewis, did not marry until late in life. Lewis was nearly sixty years of age when he married. He died at sixty-five, after the death of his wife. Lewis' life as a young man was dissolute before his conversion.

Christians have sometimes given up marriage because of the unsatisfactory character of their lives before they made spiritual commitment. It appears the Soren Kierkegaard, the Danish philosopher, may have refused marriage because of his guilt over one sexual act as a young man. Kierkegaard died at the age of 42. Had he lived longer, he might have forgiven himself sufficiently to have married.

Singles occupy a large segment of the total population. According to Marie Edwards, coauthor of "The Challenge of Being Single," there were, in the mid-1970s, 43 million single adults over 18 in America. About 10 million were widows, another two million widowers. The rest were either divorced or never married. "And that," said Edwards, "is a population large enough to defend itself against the traditional stigma attached to singles."[1] The 1970 United States census includes statistics on the marital status of persons over 18 years of age. Nineteen percent of the men and nearly 14 percent of the women were unmarried and had never married. The separated, widowed or divorced included nearly 9 percent of the men and 21 percent of the women. These figures mean that in 1970, 28 percent of the males, and nearly 35 percent of the females were single.

And the percentage of singles is increasing. Between 1964 and 1974 the increase in single women between ages 14-21 was 321 percent; between 25-34, 241 percent; between 35-64, 35 percent; and 65 and older, 68 percent.[2] Even though singles are increasing in percentage and influence in

the general society, they may not be increasing proportion-
ately in the church. A Gallup Poll survey showed that,
"married persons have a better attendance record than singles" in the church.[3]

Many of the interests and problems of all singles are
similar, whether those persons are Christians or not. There
are, of course, specific differences between Christians and
non-Christians, and where an issue concerns only Christian
singles we will select our examples only from Christians. It is
better to use incomplete evidence than to rely entirely upon
opinions, even those of the most popular and accepted
Christian counselors. We do not yet have sufficient statistical
information about singles, and much of what is available is
contradictory.

What should the single person's attitude be toward marriage? He will presumably be happier with his present and
future marital status if he seriously reviews the implications
of both his options. Should he remain single? Or should he
marry? These first chapters will ask the single reader to
seriously consider the possibility of remaining single.

THE OPTIONS

The single person has the choice of remaining single or
getting married. Christian marriage, when properly understood, will seem as foreign to many single persons as the
environment of the moon is to the earth. Similarities to the
average marriage are less important than the dynamic differences. Civil marriage, common law marriage, "living together" and other cultural forms such as levirate marriage in
the Bible are quite different from what we mean by a Christian marriage. Our concern is only with two basic options,
the Christian single life style and Christian marriage.

Marriage for the Christian is a creative act of God, provided for man during the period of God's creative activity in
the Garden of Eden. Christian marriage is reviewed in the
latter portion of Ephesians 5. The basic content of that passage describes the roles of the husband and wife in a marriage. A husband is presumed to be the Christ-figure in the

home. All that Christ would do for the church, his bride, a husband is to do for his wife as his part in the analogy. And all that the church is expected to do in relationship to Christ, the wife is to do for her husband to complete her part.

According to Galatians 3:28, male and female are equals, but as equals they accept particular duties related to their separate role assignments. The children in a home are equal to their parents, but for a development or growing up period take subordinate roles to them. In the roles of father, mother, and child the Christian family should provide an analogy to Christ, the church, and the individual (convert). As the child is nurtured, the convert is discipled. In relationships which develop dynamically within the family system, Christians are expected to learn about and practice Christian virtues and ideals.

Those men and women of faith who do not wish to build a marriage relationship like that described in Ephesians are not required to do so. They may remain single and find other legitimate and wholly appropriate ways for practicing and proving their Christian lives. But to remain single is difficult, what with the general attitudes, pressures and concerns of a family-oriented society which coerce the unmarried. And singles may create their own problems.

DISTORTIONS—SPECIAL EXPERIENCES

The single state may be distorted. A person's view of the single life may be influenced by *special experiences*. Those who have been divorced, who have lived in a "common law" relationship, who have had unhappy sex experiences, or who are currently living through a trying marriage may have very strong feelings against marriage—or any other kind of commitment to another human being.

Failure in an intimate relationship or abnormal contact with others can cause us difficulties in our efforts to relate to members of the opposite sex. Dr. Sally Slocum, an exotic San Francisco dancer in 1965 under the name of "Autumn Lee," returned to the city in 1975 to present a research paper to a scholarly society on the relationships between dancers and men in bars. She worked five years in San Francisco's North Beach sex houses while attending the University of California. Ultimately she earned a Doctor of Philosophy degree. According to a leading newspaper: "She said it took her five years afterward before she could look a man straight in the face without the feeling she saw only lust. For two years, she refused to wear anything even vaguely sexy."[4]

Her research revealed that women dancers were ambivalent about themselves, their work and the men they met. They defended their work even though they felt uneasy about what they did. They assumed that the men in their audiences were maladjusted because they sought the stimulation of exotic entertainment. The dancers were seldom interested in marriage, but they did not think the single life was normal.

In another situation a woman whose views on most issues were those of the average American said she would not feel comfortable dating or marrying because a man had once forced her to participate in an act of sexual intercourse. It was rape. In counseling sessions she said that she was not afraid of men, but was repulsed by them, especially those in her generation. Her mind was closed to marriage, and she felt neither regret nor irritation about the issue. She had numerous women friends of all ages, felt no homosexual tendencies, and believing she needed to change her attitude had accepted dates with men on several occasions. The dating experiences were unsatisfactory. The young woman attended church, held a lucrative job, kept a nice apartment and believed herself to be sufficiently fulfilled. She had seen several psychiatrists about her tensions concerning men, but treatment was unsuccessful. She was told, however, that if she was basically happy there was no immediate compelling reason for her to change her status. In four or five years she might "wear out" the present attitude. If the right man entered her life the fears might disappear.

DISTORTIONS—FAMILY INFLUENCE
One's view of the single life is often influenced by *family*

experiences. Most parents "teach" their children to anticipate marriage. The questions parents ask, the assumptions they make and the remarks they relay about marriage to growing children settle the issue *for* them. This is known as "intentional training." Almost no one is prepared by his family to live as a single person.

There is little "intentional training" which prepares a person to consider his options when he becomes an adult. On the contrary, mothers too often nag their daughters into marriage, and some send them to college less for an education than to meet future husbands. Fathers sometimes insinuate that their sons or daughters are not sexually normal if they pass their mid-twenties without getting married. Even with "intentional training" those who marry sometimes complain that they were unprepared by home or school or church for marriage. The whole effort too often seems to be to "marry off" children without adequately preparing them for the experience.

For those who do not marry, there is even less preparation for life. They must learn on their own how to build a satisfying and meaningful life style. Unsatisfactory preparation for single status causes many unmarrieds to feel uncertain about themselves. They may become critical of that status and wonder why no one cares for them, or wonder if they are selfish and unable to make a meaningful life commitment. This identity crisis may be difficult to resolve. Robert R. Bell wrote on this aspect: "Conjugal life with its stress on ego needs is probably more important and more basic to American culture than to almost any other culture in the world. To be unloved in the United States is to be more than unwanted; it is to lack importance in the eyes of a 'significant other'; it is to be unchosen. This is often extremely upsetting in a culture in which being chosen is often equated with having social worth as a human being."[5]

DISTORTIONS—PREJUDICE
One's view of the single life may be affected by prejudice. Singles encounter general prejudice. Jokes about "bache-

lors" and "old maids" are commonplace. Even the names of singles sometimes suggest unhappy and drab circumstances. Apparently "spinster" came from the occupation of spinning which was dominated by women, married and single, several centuries ago. In the course of history the word was attached to women who were unmarried. One source provided the following adjectives relating to "spinster": "ardent, unpredictable, resigned, anemic, withered, hopeless, contented, man-shy, miserable." Perhaps only two of the nine words would be interpreted as attractive— "ardent" and "contented." And both have been challenged by some analysts as inappropriate to the unmarried.

It is not our purpose here to analyze prejudice. But reflection on it ought to prove helpful. Prejudice is sometimes a reaction to personal embarrassment or a way to justify unsatisfactory attitudes and conduct. It is at its worst when the object of prejudice believes it. To eradicate prejudice is almost impossible. It has its seat in the human condition. And everyone at some time or other is an object of prejudice.

The most common prejudices are those directed against the young and the old, women in middle age, the obese and the short of stature, racial minorities in a geographical area, the long haired and the bald, farmers and garbage collectors, the poorly educated and the well educated, childless couples and the parents of large families.

Directing several prejudices against one person may create almost intolerable situations. In *The Pyramid Climbers*, Vance Packard observes that the worst status of all is that of a bachelor beyond the age of 36. The unattached male faces suspicions of being a lecher, of being unwilling to make a marriage commitment, of being a homosexual. He is approaching the unhappy middle years of a lonely life and a slow decline to the end of his occupational career.

Prejudices are constructed of ignorance and pride. Ignorance is expressed by stereotyping. Pride is expressed through the belief that all, or nearly all, persons should identify their human natures in the same way, "my way." Some crude and thoughtless marrieds act as if they are morally superior simply because they are married. Similarly some singles have presumed their status to be superior. But the Scriptures clearly state that the person who marries does well and the one who remains single also does well. Each state requires its own special gifts and insights.

The way you respond to ridicule may provide clues about your own self-acceptance. The single person may rise above prejudice. He may recognize human weaknesses and become sophisticated enough to refuse to be offended by unthinking, unflattering remarks. There are blacks of my acquaintance who feel genuinely sorry for persons prejudiced against the black race. If everyone who experienced prejudice would respond to his tormentors in that spirit, but never yield on truth, the evils of prejudice might decline. The single person, like others who are objects of prejudice, is often overly sensitive. Each "old maid" or "bachelor" tale is taken as a personal affront.

But the single person may also join the humor, even turn the joke back on the originator. I am a bald man and I know many jokes on baldness. I have sometimes been the object of the fun. In that way I find many anecdotes which I use later. I have been asked what polish I use on my pate, what wig I would prefer (I have even been presented a "toupee" made from pancake batter and straw!), and what office I would like to hold in an organization called the "chrome domes." I have been asked to consider the use of a hairpiece. I am frankly not troubled or embarrassed by the remarks. I find myself quite at ease and get more laughs when I tell stories about bald men than men with hair ever could. There is strong reason to believe that if singles could take themselves less seriously, join in the merriment or turn a potential insult into a joke, they might cease to feel they are treated without empathy. A sense of humor disarms potential tormentors.

CONCLUSION—INTENTIONAL TRAINING

Your view of the single life should begin with your own personhood, not with your marital status. To be a person is more important than to be single or married. You are a person before your sexuality makes any difference. As small children we begin to sense we are individuals among other individuals. Gradually we become aware that some of us are boys and some of us are girls—and it might have taken longer if our parents hadn't emphasized the fact! Small girls are trained for marriage by playing with dolls, dishes, playhouses and home nursing kits. Boys are provided a much wider range of playthings which prepare them for professional life. Little wonder that women feel they are pushed into marriage and domesticity, while men do not feel this push as acutely.

In consultations with husbands and wives a counselor often finds wives fail to understand the stresses and strains men experience in business. And wives feel husbands have little understanding of the problems of domestic life. Neither sex has been adequately educated to identify with the daily life of the other. Little wonder then that men and women who work together often develop romantic attachments for each other. They feel that they are understood, that they share mutual and meaningful tasks.

When most married couples lived on farms, the sharing of the farm experience was salutary to marriage. Husband, wife and child worked together in a common environment. They sensed their unity, their need for each other and mutual dependence. Single children, brothers, uncles, aunts, cousins were often equal and accepted members of households.

Today's parents should rear their children to consider the possibility of being single. Children should be taught that marriage fulfills a different set of goals and meets certain human needs. They should know that they may choose to be single, follow a pattern of interests and fulfill needs which are somewhat different from those of married people. Singles will relate more intensely to their blood families, maintain broader, less intimate friendships and find fulfillment in their work and general activities. Their greatest adjustment problem in society will be to live in a world designed to cater primarily to husband, wife and dependent child.

CHAPTER TWO

Spiritual Motivation For Singles

Some are incapable of marriage from birth, some
are made incapable by the action of men, and some
have made themselves so for the sake of the
kingdom of Heaven. Let the man who can accept
what I have said accept it. (Matthew 19:12 Phillips)

Singles may distort their perceptions about marriage. Distortions sometimes begin for men with misunderstandings about women. And misunderstanding is extensive, going far beyond marriage and family roles. The role of women in the life and ministry of the church was significantly different in the early centuries of the Christian era, when women were often leaders, from what it is perceived to be in our time.

Even in ancient and patriarchal times, as described in the Old Testament, there were leading women, good and evil, like Miriam, Deborah, Esther, Jezebel and Athaliah. Women were commonly consulted and their influence was significant, as illustrated in the lives of Sarah, Rebekah and Rachel. The influence of Rahab and Ruth is recalled in the lineage of David. Both Ruth and Esther have Old Testament books named after them. During some cycles in history, including Jewish and church history, women were less influential than in other cycles. Sometimes they were degraded; sometimes they were elevated. In some cultures segregating women apparently reduced the opportunity for sexual misconduct on the part of either sex. And the harshness of life had something to do with devices (such as isolation and veiling) which were used to protect women and children. Those devices appear unsatisfactory by modern standards.

Jesus showed unusual concern for women, often used them in his parables, and included women as well as male disciples in his preaching missions. With all that Jesus said favorably about marriage, he gave greater importance to love for God and discipleship. In Matthew 19 the Pharisees wanted to debate with Jesus on marriage because he apparently did not share their view of marriage nor their attitude toward women.

At the time of Jesus marriage may have been the most sacred Jewish institution. When Jesus suggested that marriage is indissoluble, even the disciples questioned the wisdom of choosing marriage. Jesus answered that there is the privilege of the single state which might be appropriate for several reasons. This shocked the Jews who heard it. Jesus gave new honor to the unmarried.

The Jews believed marriage was a commandment, not something merely permitted. For this reason they made marriage prerequisite to holding membership or office in important groups like the Sanhedrin. This would provide cause for hating eunuchs (castrated males), those physically unfit for marriage. However Isaiah 56:4-5 honors eunuchs for spiritual reasons.

The word translated *eunuch* appears in only one passage in the New Testament—Acts 8, the story of the conversion of the Ethiopian eunuch. Since he was a eunuch in the service of a queen, we presume he was single. He is represented as a sophisticated man. We know him to be black-skinned, in that he was an Ethiopian, and he appears to have been noble in character. He is, to our knowledge, the first black convert to Christianity. (As an aside, it is interesting that the Bible presents many people who have often been the targets of prejudice as superior to the ordinary population. Women, for example, are seldom placed in a bad light in the New

Testament Scriptures, and even prostitutes were placed above the religious Pharisees in one of Jesus' discourses. On the four or five occasions in which black people are cited in the Bible, they appear to be noble.)

The word *eunuchs* appears in the New Testament only in Matthew 19:12, one verse. Few expositors insist that the literal meaning of castration applies in Jesus' use of the word. Some translations drop the word "eunuch" for a word meaning "singles." Most writers point out the option of celibacy to marriage presented here by Jesus. A. W. Argyle, in *The Cambridge Bible Commentary on Matthew*, states: "Clement of Alexandria [wrote], 'The true eunuch is not he who cannot, but he who will not indulge himself.'" Even some of the ancients perceived that Jesus referred to singles rather than mutilated male servants.

SINGLES AND CHRISTIAN DUTY

Singles should recognize that the biblical injunctions apply to everyone. Jesus gave no place to sexism, nor did he provide advantage or disadvantage to persons married or single. The only complete exposition about the unmarried in the Bible appears in I Corinthians 7, where the word *unmarried* appears four times. Paul says not only that the single state is honorable but that the unmarried should seriously consider remaining so. The thrust of the passage is that Christians are to serve Christ intently and fully. Whether single or married, the individual is to perform at a high level.

All Christians are asked to be devoted *stewards*. Each should possess a sacrificial spirit. It has been asserted that church tithers and those who contribute most to special causes are likely to be married. If this generosity on the part of those who are married is motivated only by concern for a formal ministry to one's own family, the honor is somewhat reduced. But if giving is motivated by a love for God, the sacrificial spirit should be equally represented among Christian singles. Certainly many singles give liberally, but taken as a group the percentage contributions of singles appear to be lower than marrieds. Some argument has been offered that singles may find that more than the usual amount of money is needed to fund personal activities and experiences which substitute for home and fireside. Singles often do not feel obligated to support, either personally or financially, the institutional church program.

All Christians are urged to develop *relationships*. So all should include persons in their lives. The absence of mate and children in one's life does not free a person from the duty to develop special and honorable relationships with marrieds and singles, and with children.

And the sexual identity of these friends is basically unimportant. My own experience provides evidence to support larger social bonds. I am married but have numerous single friends who are special to me. If I interpret their gestures and conversation correctly, they feel the same way about me. Many of these singles are aunts and uncles to children, and only a few of the children are real nieces and nephews. Two single men among my friends have served as babysitters to one of my grandsons and have taken him to special programs as well as out to dinner. The lad loves and admires these men. They are proud of their "uncle" relationship to him. Their involvement is not the expression of unrequited love in their lives.

All Christians are urged to involve themselves in some form of *leadership*. Everyone should be given an opportunity to practice his gifts. In most of the singles groups I have known, leadership has been exercised by marrieds or singles who were formerly married. The most successful ones have had married or pastoral leadership. And the vastly greater number of pastors serving singles were married. On occasion the singles, all of whom were adults, functioned like full-grown children guided by elder parent figures. At the same time, some singles who have attempted leadership with singles groups have complained that they were frustrated with their assignments because singles are not loyal to a program and cannot be counted upon to support it. The mobility of singles, the appeal of the nomadic life makes solid work with singles difficult. It appears that singles are generally more fully committed to married leadership for themselves than leadership from singles.

By choosing married leadership, singles imply that a marriage background is more appropriate for administration. But if this were necessarily the case, we would not give high marks to the leadership of the Apostle Paul, or the Apostle John, or any other single. The Apostle Paul made reference to Peter's wife in noting that he too could have taken a wife. No difference in spiritual authority is attributed to the difference in marital state between the two apostles. In the Book of Acts the four daughters of Philip were said to be evangelists. We may assume that they were single; otherwise they would likely have been identified with the names of their husbands rather than their father. Doubtless, others listed as colleagues with Paul were single and active as leaders. The names referred to in Romans 16, appear to be well mixed between men and women, singles and marrieds. The impact made by the chapter is that persons, most of whom were common citizens in the larger community, had become leaders in the Christian church regardless of their marital status. Their work and devotion commended them, not their ages, sex or marital status.

All Christians are urged to live *righteously*. Everyone should be committed to righteous living. How does this relate to human sexual passion? Even many Christian singles insist that they have the right to sexual experience with members of the opposite sex. Nearly all defense of sexual expression for Christian singles in heterosexual relationships comes from males. One wrote that celibacy in singles "is naive and antagonistic to a basic gift from God." He said this denial would "subhumanize unmarrieds."[7] Another single wrote: "I take exception to the idea that remaining single in the New Testament necessarily means being celibate. As to Jesus and Paul, there is much about them we just do not know ... Jesus, theologically, had to be a real man, which would include sexual nature and expression."[8]

The basic response to these views is that Jesus clearly approves of sexual expression with someone of the opposite sex only within a marriage. Sexual intercourse between a man and woman was, in fact, equivalent to marriage, even if the woman was a harlot. And no action of Jesus in the Gospels could be interpreted as a possible violation of his celibacy. In the Scripture the condemnation of "fornication" is clearly a strong argument against sexual activity for singles. Intercourse between two persons married, but not to each other, constitutes "adultery." All extramarital intercourse, including intercourse between two unmarried people, is "fornication." The New Testament is clear about the matter.

The Apostle Paul opens the seventh chapter of I Corinthians with the warning that it is an unrighteous act for an unmarried man to touch a woman with sexual intent. The unmarried state is implied in the whole text. But if anyone wants physical intimacy, marriage is the exclusive environment in which it may take place. This privilege is not the only benefit or responsibility of marriage, but it is important to the whole context of marriage.

Further, the Scripture suggests that sexual sins have a special effect, that one does not simply sin against God and others when he commits sexual sins but against himself. If anyone, Christian or non-Christian, wants to defend the freedom of sexual expression, he may have the freedom to do so, but he does not have biblical support for his view. The whole impression of Scripture is that to be single is to practice celibacy. Any other point of view must originate and be defended from some other source, usually contemporary secular thought and practice.

All Christians are urged to participate in the *ministry*. Everyone should include service in his life. In I Corinthians 7 the Apostle Paul asserted that ministry is important enough to cause some Christians to remain single in order to give more time to their Christian ministry than a married person can ordinarily do.

Some singles have protested that this pattern places an unfair burden upon them, robbing them of familial privileges and imposing a greater responsibility on their shoulders. The protest relies upon a misconception of the spiritual life. From a human viewpoint there may be inequities, but service is for Christ's sake, not for the purpose of balancing human activity. There is quite a difference between the effort of many ministers and missionaries who choose to give up wealth and privilege—even health—for Christ's sake, and many Christian laymen who choose to devote their lives to standard secular employment and reap the rewards which accrue from that choice. A small number of people in the Christian ministry also become affluent. In the final day the first shall be last and the last first. It is in this light that one should make his own decision before God, without concern for the dedication or lack of it in another Christian, married or unmarried.

As a matter of fact, it appears that some persons may serve Christ better married and others unmarried. The point is to serve fully in whatever state one finds himself or chooses to follow. We have already learned that one state is not to be honored or preferred above another. Both are given of God. Both are guided by Scripture.

CHAPTER THREE

Self-Assessment For Singles

I would like you to be free from worry. An unmarried man concerns himself with the Lord's work, because he is trying to please the Lord. But a married man concerns himself with worldly matters, because he wants to please his wife.
(1 Corinthians 7:32-33 GNB)

Publications often repeat facts that recur among unmarried people in the general population. Dr. Harold Prince refers to a researcher who asked a general sample of unmarried, professionally educated women over 35 why they had not married. Their answers, in order of frequency, were: 1) marriage would compete with career goals; 2) there seemed to be no opportunity to meet eligible men; 3) marriage would compete with other values they held; 4) they felt inadequate to the demands of marriage; 5) a lack of interest in men; and 6) hereditary or health factors.

Another investigator found the following traits in single women: 1) unattractiveness; 2) masculine mannerisms; 3) unsocial and aggressive behavior; 4) rigidity of personality; and 5) moodiness.

One researcher asked a sample of adults, most of whom were women, to describe the personal and social characteristics of unmarried men over 35 whom they knew and to indicate whether they thought these men were marriageable. Less than 30 percent of the bachelors were considered marriageable. The others were described as being too conceited and self-centered, or too attached to their mothers.[9]

Responses from Christians show a similar range in the attitudes of and about singles. Married people often confess that they have not thought much about singles. They think unmarried people can take care of themselves because they are not distracted by family duties. Others believe that unattached men and women are a threat to marrieds. One wrote: "It might help if single males and females would try to understand the threat they are to married people."[10]

Responses from Christians, some marrieds and many singles, especially from unmarried women, repeated some of the criticisms found in the research of the general population. Many marrieds said there were significant differences represented among the singles they knew and observed in their churches. They were generally agreed that happy singles accepted themselves and were committed to God. These Christian singles were happy because they were free of competition and found themselves developing their own roles, living them to the full. They did not confuse their situations with the life choices of others.

POLARIZATION AMONG SINGLES

Counselors have discovered four groups of attitudes toward marriage among singles. *Some singles wish to marry as a matter of preference.* Most of these will. Whatever their state may be in the future, they proceed with their jobs and involve themselves in society. While single they may dream, even fantasize, about marriage, but they survive and refuse to lose the benefits of living because they are not married. They ultimately resolve the issue of their marital state and are at peace. Society and the Christian community benefit by their contributions.

Some singles intend to marry at any cost. They will accept mates significantly different in culture and conduct in order to be married. They will sacrifice their morals, their integrity and even their faith in order to get married. Unhappiness, disillusionment and failure commonly follow. And life may never get on track again. Religious partners in such ill-formed marriages encounter many problems which ministers are often called upon to help solve. This is a major issue. Ministers often see it coming before the marriage is solemnized. Being single was unacceptable but marriage became impossible. One psychiatrist stated: "I am sometimes tempted to think that half of my patients are neurotic because they are married and the other half because they are not!"

Some singles maintain their status as singles, but expect the companionship of members of the opposite sex. They may seek sexual companionship and domestic privileges without assuming full responsibility for either their acts or the persons from whom they receive these services. This conduct is sometimes justified because of "mutual consent." Mutual consent is presumed to set aside the moral issues. At best, mutual consent deals only with the legality of the acts, not with their morality. Much that is legal is immoral. Tension has arisen between Christian singles themselves over the collision of views relative to singles and sex. I assume that the majority of serious Christian singles oppose intimate sexual activity outside of marriage. Sometimes the license of many non-Christians and some Christians influenced by the Playboy/Playgirl philosophy is unfairly seen as characteristic of all Christian singles. Christian unmarrieds may need to develop and publicize a critique of the "swinging" life style, just as Christian marrieds must disavow the pagan distortions of marriage.

Some singles are determined to remain single at any cost. For some people the unmarried life is fulfilling and happy. They counteract those stereotypes which are sometimes used to characterize singles. However, many determine to remain single because they dislike or distrust that half of the human race represented by the opposite sex. Norman Bradburn, working with the National Opinion Research Center of the University of Chicago, found single men to be the unhappiest of all persons in American society. He discovered that single women are most satisfied with their choice to remain unmarried. We do not know if some persons are unhappy because they are single or remain single because they are unhappy. We do know that many married persons are deeply unhappy, and that many singles are happy. Too little is known about happy singles.

RESPONSIBILITY AMONG SINGLES

Singles may need to evaluate their sense of responsibility. Many singles withdraw from *involvement* in society. (So do some marrieds.) Some withdrawal is due to shyness, an affliction shared by many marrieds. Shy persons may not have the emotional resources to involve themselves, to carry their fair share of the load nature places upon all of us. Everyone should "pay his dues." There is a basic investment to be made by all members of the human race, married or single. In a sense, schools, neighboring families, government and other institutions are partly my responsibility, even if I never have children, never own property and never ask quarter in society. One does not secede from the human race simply because he will not experience everything his fellow members experience.

Selfishness is not so easily disguised for singles as it is for marrieds. A married couple may be selfish. The attitudes of a husband and wife may be misinterpreted as love and devotion. If a man and wife have no children they may dote on one another. Observers may believe they are in love when as a matter of fact they may be basically selfish. Singles have no such easy or acceptable hedge.

Single men who do not marry are sometimes still accused of numerous personal and moral failures. Philip Roth summarized one set of accusations about the bachelor: ". . . he was just plain 'selfish.' Or he was 'frightened of responsibility.' Or he could not 'commit himself' (nice institutional phrase, that) to a 'permanent relationship.' Worst of all, most shameful and humbling of all, chances were he was a person who was 'unable to love.'"[11] Roth challenged this concept. He believed that much of the feeling about bachelors was generated by women who, because of their larger numbers, had to have as many male candidates for marriage as possible. He felt some men were shamed into marriage when they should have remained single.

Many women are also pressed into marriage. A young woman reflected to the syndicated column, "Dear Abby," that she was determined to pursue law as a career, was a straight "A" student, was not physically attractive nor popular. She said her father was critical of her and accused her of latent homosexuality. She wrote: "I really don't care about having a husband and a herd of kids, and there is no way I will spend my life being a housewife. I'd crack up."[12] If the young woman is selfish, one might like to assist her in recognizing her weakness. However, if her affirmations for education, career, service to those about her and worthy life goals were greater than her negations about originating a family unit, her protestations would not be as selfish as the stark words make her appear.

A person may become attached to himself, and whether he is aware of it or not he becomes wizened and lonely. Karl Olsson wrote about a new fad he read about—"monosexuality, which means being hooked on yourself . . . and if you don't want to submit yourself to the bondage and the freedom of a life together [in marriage], why not go it alone?"[13] And Olsson stated that a judge had married a monosexual to himself.

This peculiar ceremony is not to be confused with those services of dedication in which one or more singles are presented to God and the congregation affirming their devotion to Christ and his standards for life and service. Such a service is a celebration of the life of God in singles. The singles do not necessarily promise *never* to marry, but to serve fully and gladly in the state God has given them at the moment.

Singles may attempt to avoid *social responsibility*. They do not vote as often as their married counterparts. They may shy away from office-holding, even while they complain that they receive little opportunity for high level achievements. It was discovered in one study that single collegians who are strong on protest tended to vote less often than the general populace. Although below national averages, the voting record for married collegians is better than that for single collegians.

A common complaint of singles is that they carry a disproportionate tax burden. At this writing, singles do pay higher taxes than marrieds. And the direct personal return for those tax dollars is lower for singles. There is a national organization dedicated to gaining legislation to equalize taxes between marrieds and singles. It is known simply as CO$T, with a dollar sign used for the "S" in CO$T. The initials stand for the Committee of Single Taxpayers. Lobbying efforts have been rebuffed during first attempts. It is not likely that taxes will be equalized for all groups because of the graduated income tax principle which places the larger burden on those who are presumed to have the greater ability to pay. Property owners pay taxes to support public schools even if they have no children. The awareness of community more than the awareness of individual rights alone will have some bearing on how taxes are determined. In some way the social responsibility of each person must be computed and carried.

Singles may follow a more discriminating personal pattern of spending than marrieds. They possess greater financial independence. And some singles are paid more for their labor than is commonly thought. Despite lower average incomes for singles than for marrieds, single women after years of experience are likely to be paid more than married women who move in and out of the work force. Alfred Prince states: "In 1960 middle-aged women with incomes of more than $10,000 were less likely to have married than those with incomes under $5,000."[14] And with laws banning discrimination, the professional opportunities and rewards for labor are improving for singles. This is demonstrated by the ease in which singles take jobs and quit them, in the movement from community to community, in the choice of life style.

FRUSTRATIONS AMONG SINGLES

Singles need to confront frustration. Elsewhere and in another context I mention the four major complaints of singles: continuing loneliness, omission of sex and parenthood, concealment of human emotions, and disappointment with status.[15]

Loneliness is, many writers agree, the most significant frustration singles must endure. No other complaint is mentioned as often. Following the first passionate years of adult life, not even sexual suppression is close as the second problem. Nearly all of us want to be close to at least one other person. For most of us that person is a parent, a spouse or a child of our own. But substitutes are available. Life is full of good friends if one is willing to make them. And many persons have full lives in their own private company. They generally find a balance between self-discovery and the discovery of others.

Is a recluse lonely? Is the person who erects barriers to friendship lonely? Likely they are. But they would be lonely even if they were to marry, and marriage would merely add other problems. I know one such person well. Lonely because she withdraws from others, she is suspicious of her outgoing husband. She attributes ill motives to him. Her misery is heightened by marriage, her loneliness at least as great as if she were single.

The number of adult singles increased abruptly during the decade of the 1970s. Complaints about loneliness significantly subsided. Increasingly, independent single life was perceived as an appropriate, perhaps even lengthy, transition period between the end of living with parents and beginning marriage. More persons spoke of marriage coming to them in their late twenties or early thirties. Career development was seen by many women as a substitute for marriage. Working with scintillating colleagues was enough to satisfy their need for friendship; and quiet, independent evenings in "one's own digs" was seen as a benefit. Men and women living alone cite freedom and independence as the great advantages. Many dropped their roommates of the same sex, not to become "swingers" but to truly live "alone." Sales of condominiums significantly increased among singles. For some the style has been self-indulgent, but for many there is a happy and fulfilling experience of self-discovery and fulfillment.

Singles have a strong need to cope with their *sex drives*. Those drives have not always been as intense as the current generation may think. Studies of native societies show that sex is not as all-encompassing as the Western world has made it. In a society which cannot sell automobile batteries or toothpaste without appealing to prurient interests, the sublimation of the drive is difficult. Our sexual appetites are assaulted daily. Desire and passion are intensified. Compulsion and urge rest heavily upon the mass of the population. And there appears no way out.

Analysts are becoming increasingly aware of the extent to which the sex drive is mental rather than physical. We know much of current interest in sex in America is rooted more in the psychology than in the physiology of man. Some generations have overly suppressed sexual activity and even sexual discussion; others have overly expressed themselves. The mass media's violation of intimacy in sex has opened a Pandora's box. Everyone is titillated. The pattern provides temptations which may be insurmountable for many singles, and even marrieds. Either or both may be caught up in illicit sex.

If a man or woman can find sexual partners, it is likely that he or she can find marriage partners and act in responsible ways. Those who are unable to find marriage partners will not easily discover sex partners who will be interested in them as persons. Promiscuous men and women are identifiable. The real choice for a Christian is not one of promiscuity but of marriage or celibacy. You can be scintillating without losing your integrity. And letting down your moral standards does not make you scintillating. Mature persons are perfectly capable of indicating an interest in each other that will lead to marriage before it is expressed sexually.

It is likely that women, who are not yet permitted socially

to take the initiative in making marriage proposals, are partly compensated by greater self-control in sex. Women appear to find substitutes for marriage and sex more readily than men. They are more willing than men to delay marriage, more likely to find satisfaction in a meaningful occupation and not marry at all if a prospective marriage threatens their careers. Even though some women's liberationists protest alleged differences in the sexual intensities of men and women, present evidence suggests that the desires of men are stronger than those of women and that men express themselves sexually more often than women.

According to many observers, singles are troubled about their *status*. They find doors of opportunity closed to them because, without marriage, they are presumed to be less responsible, a potential threat to the solidarity of marriage among their peers, and perenially passing through puberty. (This last is accented by the Playboy philosophy.) In a family-centered society the absence of a wife and children places the single man at a disadvantage in any race for professional or political prizes. And it may be that without the responsibility of a family and home he is less competitive in the business world. According to L. M. Boyd, "Statistically, a man is almost three times more likely to be successful in his career if he is married, say the scholars."[16]

The *concealment of feeling* is another major problem for singles. The single person often cannot express his feelings as a married person does. Social life for singles is different. It is not easy for them to talk about many of the things married people talk about. The focus of society is on homes, children and mates, with all the social accoutrements of family life, including family vacations and schooling. Singles may be forced to live in a different world, a world where silence may be compelled except when they are drawn together in their own cadres. One form of this concealment is discussed by Paul Tournier:

> I know that for every normal woman who as
> the years go by sees her hope of marriage
> evaporating, spinsterhood is a terrible trial,

and one the acceptance of which can never be
final; it is always likely to reappear in the most
painful form. Other sorrows, such as the tragic
death of a husband, wife, or child, are also
ineffaceable. But they can at least be freely
expressed, and they arouse ready sympathy.
The spinster has to conceal her sorrow. If she
allows it to show she may have to suffer mock-
ery and the sort of pleasantry to which people
are so inclined as soon as any allusion is made
to matters of sex. Or else she brings upon
herself facile and wounding advice, such as
"You have just got to accept it." Or perhaps the
stinging reply of some married women: "You
should consider yourself lucky! You can do
whatever you want—no children to worry
about, no selfish husband to kowtow to.
You've got a good income and can do what you
like with your money."[17]

ENCOURAGEMENT FOR SINGLES
What may be said about the common frustrations of singles?
First, recognize that the complaints of marrieds are surprisingly similar to those of singles. Counseling sessions with
married couples are dominated by recitations by one or both
partners of loneliness caused by neglect, absenteeism or lack
of communication. A very large percentage choose divorce
in the belief that loneliness alone is better than loneliness
married.

Second, sexual frustration and conflict are so common
among marrieds that some counselors presume that all marital difficulties are affected by sexual differences between
husband and wife. Counselors who work with large numbers of both married and single clients may find more sexual
frustration and complaint in exchanges with marrieds than
with singles. Some prostitutes report that nearly all their
customers are married, which would be surprising if marriage adequately meets their sexual needs.

On the matter of concealment of feelings, the issue is almost entirely determined by the kind of social life one chooses. Majority groups tend to dominate. Because marrieds dominate population statistics, their interests and patterns will dominate. Marrieds who move among singles, when singles dominate, also find themselves out of the mainstream of conversation. Laborers outnumber supervisors in the general population. But the lowly worker in the presence of ten supervisors in a plant will likely feel some reticence under the circumstances. And he will sense some loss of whatever status he ordinarily possesses. One who has been in the academic world has observed what happens when a person without scholarly pedigree tries to maintain himself in the presence of colleagues who have completed terminal degrees. The illustrations could be multiplied.

Many marrieds presume the single state to be attractive enough to seek divorce in order to restore that state. The better state is probably in the eye of the beholder. The problems of singles, all very real, are the problems, in one form and intensity or other, of most other human beings. They are problems of the human condition.

The opinion of Paul Tournier, that "every normal woman" struggles with spinsterhood, and by implication, every single male with bachelorhood, is not necessarily true. His description of those who *are* deeply troubled by their situations and have no recourse is excellent. But many are untroubled because they have never accepted the idea that the fulfillment of their personhood may be found only in marriage.

Christians, single or married, are often in foreign and uncomfortable situations. To avoid uneasiness in those situations, some Christians abandon their habits and life style to accommodate a temporary experience. They fall into profanity or drinking in attempting to gain temporary acceptance. They may yield to sexual participation, even to marriage, against their better judgment.

Other Christians maintain themselves, accept discomfort

and emerge from the tempting experience with greater inner peace than those who accommodated themselves. The single needs to believe in himself. He should not, he must not, accommodate if to do so is a denial of his person. He has something exemplary to offer to others and to himself that is unique to his single state.

The tensions one faces are often overcome or managed when he fills the empty places of his life with appropriate conduct. It remains a mystery to counselors why lonely unhappy singles refuse even those legitimate opportunities which come to them, and reject their own creativity as a way of filling up their lives. Laziness may be a part of the problem. Christian singles do not appear to entertain socially as much as Christian marrieds do. Except for special programs such as symphony concerts or eminent speaker events, singles are less likely to appear at standard scheduled programs. The Scriptures well represent the principle: "He that hath friends must show himself friendly." Singles may invite marrieds if they are not invited by marrieds. Why must the married always initiate a friendship?

The unmarried may enjoy his deeper privacy, his long periods of being alone. If so, there should be no complaint about competing life styles. Many persons, married and unmarried, are, like Lot, looking over into Sodom, hankering for something, but in their best moments they accept the separation which God provides.

The capabilities of our minds are underestimated. Sex drives diminish significantly when the mind is employed with other matters. Other frustrations also diminish. Human appetites are controllable. Thoughts can be brought into subjection. A very large segment of the American public has done just that. Some persons who were promiscuous, and whose physical powers remain, have become celibate. Both men and women have achieved effective self-control. The possibilities are present, the opportunities are available. A willingness, even a deep desire, for the best my state can offer may have to precede the experience of that best. My life may be filled in creative ways. I should avoid laziness, for by sloth my life can be wasted. Energy, life, participation, confidence and their handmaidens will help me meet my needs.

Spiritual activity is the best of all places for meeting personal needs. I have biblical imperatives to implement in my life. I have principles to learn. Texts related to my problems guide, medicate and restore me, and "renew a right spirit within me." They provide light beams in times of darkness and gloom.

Prayer and sharing lift my spirit. Awareness of the ordeals and victories of others guide and comfort me. Out of this commitment to Christ, and out of the resources he provides, I may become an example of the victorious Christian life to anyone who will touch my life and be touched by it.

Preparing For Marriage

INTRODUCTION

*Be faithful to your own wife and give love to her
alone. Children that you have by another woman
will do you no good. Your children should grow up
to help you, not strangers. So be happy with your
wife and find your joy with the girl you
married—pretty and graceful as a deer. Let her
charms keep you happy; let her surround you with
her love. Son, why should you give your love to
another woman? Why should you prefer the
charms of another man's wife? The Lord sees
everything you do. Wherever you go, he is
watching. The sins of a wicked man are a trap. He
gets caught in the net of his own sin. He dies
because he has no self-control. His utter stupidity
will send him to his grave.(Proverbs 5:15-23 GNB)*

I am now assuming that individuals who review the
benefits and problems of single life will likely confront and
resolve the issues of marriage with greater effectiveness than
those who do not analyze both options. As noted in the
preface, marriage should become an option freely chosen,
not something that is generally expected or forced on the
individual by parents and society. Marriage ought to be the
unfettered choice of each person who marries.

Marriage solidarity confronts its greatest challenges in
affluent times. When persons are relatively free and do not
need each other for financial and social support, marriage
will be questioned, because with all its benefits it requires
much of the husband and wife. Even wealthy and religious
patriarchs like Abraham, Isaac and Jacob encountered marital difficulties. Job and his wife were at odds over several
vital issues. The Book of Job may be the oldest of all biblical

writings, and it intimates family failure in the introduction
and success in the conclusion. Ancient eminent Roman
writers—Petronius, Juvenal, Ovid and Martial—reported
marital tensions among the middle and upper classes in
ancient Rome. Married men of wealth frequented prostitutes and sometimes escaped to the bordellos of Pompeii.
The wives of leading men in Rome abandoned some of the
roles which had brought virtue and stability to the Empire
and turned to scandalous behavior. Reading the ancients
and moderns, one is persuaded that the problems of marriage have been fairly general thoughout history. Like other
social institutions, marriage encounters cycles which elevate
and depress it. The differences may reflect the quality of
persons who enter marriage in any given era. No matter
where the cycle rests in any generation, a specific marriage
may do well or fail as the members of the marriage perform
well or poorly.

Some publicity about marital problems has been common throughout the centuries, but today's media have made
them general knowledge. Popular mass forms of communication were nonexistent until recent years. Currently, then,
with public accents on the unusual and bizarre, more dam-
age than formerly may be done in denigrating marriage.
Much that is asserted is simply untrue. The prophecies of the
end of marriage, prophecies based on strident complaints of
unhappy persons formerly married, or the assertions of
experimental cohabiting couples, have been widely reported
as fact but have not come to pass. Many of the prophecies
emanate from persons who articulate fads, arguing that
these are significant cultural trends. Analysis about what is
really happening is often faulty.

Hard evidence favors marriage. Patrick McGrady, quot-
ing Dr. Eric Pfeiffer, wrote: "Researchers have discovered
that those who live the longest generally have high intelligence, financial security, good health and a good marriage.[18]
In analyzing the long lives of persons who survive to one

hundred years of age in various parts of the world, McGrady wrote: "They tend to have long, relatively happy marriages with frequent sexual activity in later years."[19] The researchers discovered that centenarians not only had strong family ties, but also were "happy in their families."

Marriage continues to be popular and, it appears, will remain so. At the turn of the twentieth century one in five Americans did not marry. Currently, about one in ten will not, although the percentages of singles appear to be increasing again. Millions are married, only thousands try substitutes for marriage. The most generous authority has said that perhaps a million out of a particular generation numbering tens of millions have tried alternatives to marriage.

The future of marriage is reflected more by the millions who participate in it than by the thousands who do not. Family-centered businesses, churches and schools flourish while exotic alternatives flounder and fade, ebb and flow. Families and traditions related to formal marriage may be expected to prevail. And it is significant that one of the Bible's favorite analogies for teaching spiritual truth is marriage and the family. That figure is strong and will remain so, especially for the Christian.

Nevertheless, marriage is characterized in America by much unhappiness. Literature in the field advances scores of reasons for the unfortunate state of affairs. Much unhappiness is the result of unrealistic expectations created by claims about what marriage is supposed to be. Expectations about money, children, status, romance and sensitivity create problems which for some couples are insoluble, or seem so. There is reason to believe premarital counseling could significantly assist in improving the future of many marriages.

One way to make marriage happy is to prepare for it. That principle holds for most human aspirations. A young person soon learns to enjoy college if he prepares his assignments. He gains satisfaction by setting goals, working out finances and studying for classes and exams. Anyone who goes to his job prepared will find it manageable and gratifying.

Marriage, too, responds to advance analysis, decision making, reflection on potential problem areas, understanding and planning. The questions which follow in the next section of the book are designed to help persons prepare for Christian marriage or improve marriages that can and should be better. Most of these questions may be answered several ways. Individual couples must determine the way that is best for their needs. Needs, interests and values vary and determine compatibility. Your temperaments, personality, backgrounds and goals will lead to different "right" answers for you than for someone else. The slang idiom, "Different strokes for different folks," says you have options. Marriage patterns are not rigid. If, however, two engaged persons agree on many issues, they may feel confident about the future of their marriage.

It should be understood that when some assertions are made in the following pages, the author is aware that there will be exceptions. A book would make dull reading if each general application were qualified. You should, therefore, understand that most statements made apply to most couples and that your case might be an exception.

Our concern in this book is in part to offer preventive measures. What you know about premarital counseling will encourage you to utilize it. Preventive medicine, taken before an illness strikes, makes sense; pre-engagement and premarital counseling before a marriage has a chance to go bad also makes sense. Each marriage may be thought of as a potential divorce, a divorce almost no couple wants to happen. Premarital counseling is a preventive technique. By it a counselor may well suggest the probable success of a prospective marriage.

How does he go about it?

A counselor working with a couple will isolate those

traits of the potential bride and groom that would tend to strengthen their relationship and those that would tend to divide them. The strength, and happiness, and even duration of a marriage can be predicted in this way. A couple might even reconsider whether they should get married at all. The fact that in the past marriage brokers in various cultures have been remarkably successful in selecting candidates for a good marriage suggests that with the additional insights of modern psychology and testing we might be expected to become even more successful.

Who should get married?

Many issues must be reviewed before that question can be answered. Those who are contemplating marriage may begin counseling at almost any point in their relationship, but the earlier the better. All couples will discover both strengthening and dividing factors. The final decision will be based on the total impression.

Important clues as to the potentially successful marriage will be found in each partner's background. L. M. Boyd has summarized those factors in an individual's background which offer a prospective bride and groom the greatest chance for a good marriage: 1) both have brothers and sisters, 2) both want the wedding in a church, 3) both lived on farms as children, 4) both like their fathers and mothers, 5) the bride-to-be has worked, and 6) both have not changed residences very often.

Your immediate response may be: "I wasn't brought up on a farm, I was an only child, my father abandoned my mother, and I have moved from one home to another. Am I never to marry?"

The answer is, "Of course you may marry, but you may have more problems to resolve than one who has had greater childhood benefits." And the best place to begin the resolution of background problems is before you get married.

The purpose of the following questions, then, is to resolve problems, secure agreements and discover those factors which will strengthen your relationship with the one you are thinking of marrying.

1. Have you talked about what you expect out of marriage?

Some Pharisees came to him and tried to trap him by asking, "Does our Law allow a man to divorce his wife for whatever reason he wishes?"
Jesus answered, "Haven't you read the scripture that says that in the beginning the Creator made people male and female? And God said, 'For this reason a man will leave his father and mother and unite with his wife, and the two will become one.' So they are no longer two, but one. Man must not separate, then, what God has joined together."
(Matthew 19:3-6 GNB)

Engaged couples, even on the eve of their marriage, have often never talked in any depth about such major topics as sex and work. You and the one you intend to marry may believe you have adequately reviewed prospective problems, but preliminary conversations in premarital counseling almost always show that couples have not. As a general rule they do not even know what questions to ask. Premarital counseling is worth the effort if it does no more than get you to think about issues you ought to consider before you begin your marriage. And sessions may lead to a breakup; that would be appropriate for many couples.

Men and women commonly differ on what they expect out of marriage. A man may view marriage as the legitimate context for sexual intimacy, as a means of meeting his sexual and other needs in an organized and moral way. He is willing to support, principally by his salary, the home and woman of his choice. He expects to give and receive love. He

senses obligations which are not always clear, but he feels he
is the protector of his future wife and children.

The woman is more likely to perceive marriage as a
source of security, a way of meeting most of her personal
needs and an opportunity to devote herself to the needs of
her husband. She presumes that he is somewhat less idealistic than she, but she feels equal to the future, hoping to
change him to adapt to her concepts. She believes she will
have to give more love than she will receive. But she is
willing to accept her situation for what she believes is a
personal and social coup. She will keep house and bear
children. She may work and participate in providing for the
family. In some ways she is more practical about the whole
matter.

The two images of marriage are unlike each other in other
ways that neither spouse fully anticipates. Those who plan
on marrying do not anticipate, and therefore do not talk
about, such specifics: moodiness, boredom, physical ap-
pearance, housekeeping, in-laws, life styles, new and former friendships, nagging and complaining, equality, goals,
personality differences, schedules, communication, mutuality, expectations and scores of other potential problems.

Engaged couples seldom think about the future development of their marriage. What will this marriage be like
in four years (the most difficult time)? How will they get
along in ten years, or when the children are gone, or when
they are old? What about those changing needs and emotions with which older marriages must cope? Couples need
to consider these potential problems at the outset of their
engagement, if not sooner. The future can be prepared for if
it is adequately understood.

There appear to be several different stages in a single
marriage. My wife and I experienced two, and we recently
entered our third. The first was a difficult period for both of
us. We experienced intimate moments of love, enjoyed our
children, followed lives of faith and service. We also experienced difficult times, misunderstandings, dislike for each

other, tensions, arguments, accusation and counter-accusation. Separation was recommended, but we rejected the option.

A turn came, partly as the result of desperation, partly because of fresh spiritual experiences in our lives. We learned *agapé* love, unselfish and other-centered, and began to practice it with each other. Twenty additional years passed. They now *seem* almost unrelated to the first section of our marriage. These twenty were idyllic, a period of growth, animation, humor, intimacy, increased service to God. The children completed their dependence and were on their own.

A new period began as the youngest child concluded her undergraduate work. Although at this writing this stage has just begun, there is for us a sense of benediction. Whatever happens, it is all right. There is no need to prove anything anymore. There is no question but that this third period is the result of the second. Had the second followed the first without radical change, there likely would not have been a third, or it would have been a miserable, silent toleration.

In a different way counselors from the Berkeley Therapy Institute found three basic stages through which most marriages move. Barbara Cady summarized them as follows:

> As relationships wear on...people become less responsive to each other's needs and wants and more resistant to each other's efforts at coercion: Stage I, the "incontestable high" characterized by mutual admiration, affectionate indulgence—and usually terrific sex—must inevitably give way to Stage II. As certain as bad breath follows garlic, the bad traits that passed unnoticed in the flush of infatuation begin to take their toll, and the couple realizes all the depressing reasons why they should never have gotten together in the first place. But beyond the anxious demands, mutual blame, pushing away and withholding

of Stage II lies hope, the authors believe, for
Stage III—a time of realistic expectations, emotional equilibrium and deepened love.[20]

If you are married or contemplating marriage, you should
remind yourself that there are several stages to be experienced in each marriage, and each needs to be prepared for in
its predecessor. If you are ready for the experiences of each
stage and can handle them, one good lifelong marriage is a
possibility for you. If these preparations or adjustments are
not made, you may end up married to several different
partners in a lifetime—the first for sex, the second for spouse
and parent, the third for social and business relationships,
and another for comforting and nursing in your declining
years. Some secular writers advise just that—to change your
marriage partners as your personal needs shift. Can anyone
believe that personal maturity could ever result from following such advice? If one partner has few gifts other than the
erotic, what purpose does he or she have during middle and
old age? And would the person whose gifts were primarily
compassion and concern be expected to wait until advanced
years to marry? The proposal is silly but it was seriously
advanced by one writer.

Someone has said that for Christians marriage is a room
with only one exit—death. The Bible does describe marriage
as a permanent lifelong relationship. A Christian man and
woman contemplating matrimony should therefore discuss
all issues in the light of this permanence. Their very commitment to the absolute quality of their marriage will assist
them in confronting their problems because they will seek
solutions elsewhere than in a divorce court.

FOR DISCUSSION:

1. Do you both perceive marriage as a lifetime commitment?
2. What does Jesus say in Matthew 19 about the permanence of marriage? What do his questioners assume
   about it?
3. Do you know any good marriages that might serve as
   models for you?

4. What has occurred in marriages among your relatives and friends that you would like to avoid in your marriage?
5. How strongly do you think your life at home as a child will influence or has influenced your own marriage?

QUESTION

2. What books have you read on marriage?

> *In the same way instruct the older women to behave as women should who live a holy life. They must not be slanderers or slaves to wine. They must teach what is good, in order to train the younger women to love their husbands, and children, to be self-controlled and pure, and to be good housewives who submit themselves to their husbands, so that no one will speak evil of the message that comes from God.*
> *(Titus 2:3-5 GNB)*

To have a good marriage you should read some of the excellent instructional material which is available. If you say you want to make your marriage work, but you are not willing to commit some time to learn how to make it work, you are not being honest. Many people enter counseling sessions who say they are sincerely eager to make their marriages work, but who refuse to read about marriage, or take basic tests, or listen to recordings.

Marriage is the most significant of all human relationships. It requires and responds to instruction. A prospective bride and groom and anyone who wants to have a better marriage should expect to study extensively in preparing for marriage.

The following books are just a few helpful ones from an extensive list on marriage and the family that should be available from your local Christian bookstore.

André Bustanoby. *You Can Change Your Personality.* Zondervan, 1976.
Charlotte H. and Howard J. Clinebell. *The Intimate Marriage.* Harper and Row, 1970.

Gary R. Collins. *It's O.K. To Be Single*. Word, 1976.

_____ . *Make More of Your Marriage*. Word, 1976.

James Dobson. *What All Wives Wish Their Husbands Knew About Women*. Tyndale, 1975.

(All of Dobson's writings are useful for family improvement.)

Elisabeth Elliot. *Let Me Be A Woman*. Tyndale, 1976.

Dale E. Galloway. *There Is A Solution to Your Money Problems*. Tyndale, 1977.

Howard G. Hendricks. *Premarital Counseling Manual*. Victor Books, 1977.

Tim and Beverly La Haye. *The Act of Marriage*. Zondervan, 1976.

Joyce Langdorf. *Tough and Tender*. Revell, 1977.

Mark W. Lee. *Creative Christian Marriage*. Regal, 1977.

_____ . *How to Make Goals and Really Reach Them*. Horizon House, 1978.

_____ . *Our Children: Our Best Friends*. Zondervan, 1970.

Evelyn and J. Allan Petersen. *For Women Only*. Tyndale, 1975.

J. Allan Petersen. *The Marriage Affair*. Tyndale, 1974.

_____ . *For Men Only*. Tyndale, 1975.

Rosalind Rinker. *How to Have Family Prayers*. Zondervan, 1977.

Letha Scanzoni. *Sex Is A Parent Affair*. Regal, 1973.

Edith Schaeffer. *Hidden Art*. Tyndale, 1975.

_____ . *What Is A Family*. Revell, 1975.

Charlie Shedd. *The Best Dad Is A Good Lover*. Sheed Andrews and McMeel, 1977.

_____ . *Talk to Me*. Doubleday, 1975.

Dwight Hervey Small. *Christian: Celebrate Your Sexuality*. Revell, 1974.

Walter Trobisch. *I Married You*. Harper and Row, 1971.

Sven Wahlroos. *Family Communication*. Macmillan, 1974.

QUESTION

3. Do you share the same religious beliefs?

> *Do not try to work together as equals with unbelievers, for it cannot be done.*
>
> (II Corinthians 6:14a GNB)

> *I want you to understand that Christ is supreme over every man, the husband is supreme over his wife, and God is supreme over Christ.*
>
> (I Corinthians 11:3 GNB)

A person's religion is important to him, even if it is non-religion. Whether your beliefs are true or false, you hold on to them. They are links to personal understanding greater than nature alone offers. Religion may assure its adherents of life after death. What could possibly be more important? Whether a person's faith is strong or weak, in God or in the stars, may not matter. Even weak faith, like an injured eye or damaged ear, appears desirable. No matter how limited in sight or hearing acuity, a person wishes to retain whatever portion of the eye or ear he may retain. A person will insist on keeping his injured arm even when it will hang limply at his side for the rest of his life.

Whatever your prospective spouse's religion, you must accept it as part of him. He will be comfortable with just that amount of faith which supports him, or anesthetizes him, or makes him acceptable to his family or friends, or truly comforts him.

Nearly all counselors raise serious questions about mixed marriages. They believe differences in faith create very basic problems which a couple ought not invite. In most mixed marriages, either the marriage or the religion becomes the casualty, but each inevitably relates in some way to the other. If a mixed marriage is going to work there will likely have to be: 1) acceptance between mates with more than ordinary qualities of understanding, sympathy, insight and creative tolerance; 2) approval of the religion or church which has the stronger allegiance; 3) agreement on what to do about the spiritual nurture of children; and 4) acknowledgement that differences about religion strike at the sensitive center of a family, and are not minor and peripheral.

During the late 1950s a study subsidized by the Harvard Social Relations Foundation and the Ford Foundation reviewed the lives of 60,000 families in various parts of the United States. The researchers, Dr. Carle C. Zimmerman and Dr. Lucius F. Cervantes, found many unhappy families. From these they made a major discovery:

> Many millions of American families have
> created a new pattern for living which is actu-
> ally a twentieth century version of the ancient
> family clan.
>
> Here is how the new clan system works:
> Each of the good and successful families sur-
> rounds itself with about five other families
> which share its ideals and many of the same
> characteristics. Usually these "friend families"
> have: the same religion, the same region of
> origin (South, Midwest, Northeast, etc.),
> approximately the same income, often a rela-
> tionship by blood or marriage.[21]

The study strongly supported the idea that these friend
families provided a sustaining wall which protected children, and presumably the adults, against some of the
world's unwholesome values. Researchers Zimmerman and
Cervantes stated: "Families having similar backgrounds,
values, interests, and outlooks with their friends show the
lowest divorce, desertion, juvenile arrest and school drop-
out rates." They pointed out that families with none of the
four traits (religion, income, region, kinship) have the worst
records.

In the section of the study which focused on interfaith marriages, the following conclusions were presented:
1) those couples with different religious affiliations have
fewer children, 2) those children are less likely to complete
high school, 3) in a Catholic-Protestant marriage six out of
ten children are likely to reject all religion, 4) the children
have a higher arrest rate, and 5) those couples with different
religious affiliations have a higher divorce rate than those
with a shared faith.

The Harvard Survey of Happy Families showed that if
neither member of the marriage belonged to a specific religious group, the desertion, divorce and delinquency rate

was four times the national average. If one spouse was religious and the other was not, the rate only doubled. This suggests that some religion in a family leads to greater family solidarity than none at all.

There are, of course, mixed marriages which are successful. But they succeed in spite of unusual hazards. In offering opinions, counselors must rely on statistics for success and failure. The official stance of all faiths, whenever an official position has been taken, is opposition to mixed faith marriages. The ministers, priests and rabbis of the various churches and synagogues have confronted numerous marital problems, all virtually insoluble, related to differences in the religions of the mates. They feel compelled to oppose a combination which has such a high failure probability. Resistance to mixed marriage is not generally related to a pastor's denominational exclusivism. After all he stands to gain on the average as many members as he loses.

Studies have been sufficiently detailed to show which combinations of religions are particularly troublesome. The greatest unhappiness and conflict, according to Dr. Judson Landis of the University of California, occur for a Catholic father and a Protestant mother.[22] In more recent polls many young persons have been questioned about their views of interfaith marriages. They tended to defend them (assuming there was a genuine love between the man and the woman) and said they would not avoid marriage just because of religious differences. However, when they were asked if they would change their religion, most said they would not. The new generation appears less practical than earlier ones which recognized the potential problems and avoided marriages which would be divisive. The experiences of young couples with a mixed religious background have been to a high degree negative. The easy collapse of such marriages suggests the impracticality of the young people polled on this issue.

Differences in religion imply other related problems

which may be expected to bombard a marriage: 1) concerns about family loyalties identified with religion, 2) disappointments felt by in-law members, 3) expectations of the children who look for uniformity in their parents' beliefs, 4) cultural differences which relate to religion and have much to do with the formation of the lives and characters of the persons involved. (For example, a person reared in a religion which is highly authoritarian will likely be a different kind of person, even it he rejects his religion, than one reared in a highly permissive religious environment.) In many ways which are not consciously related to religion, men and women act according to the conditioning of their early faith, religious or non-religious. Religion is important and cannot be disregarded if a couple wishes to build a solid foundation for future happiness. Faith changes lives and generally creates a strong bond between sincere believers.

If you differ in your religious beliefs and still insist on getting married, you greatly increase your chances for happiness and solidarity if you can amicably agree to select one church home. But when that faith is selected at the outset of a marriage there is no assurance the agreement will hold up. Some individuals may temporarily suspend their faith, but it often returns in times of personal need, more powerful than the individual ever expected. Non-Christian mates often object to the religious conversion or spiritual renewal of their partners.

FOR DISCUSSION:
1. Do you both agree on all essential aspects of your faith in God?
2. If not, how do you propose to resolve the issues?
3. If faith in Christ is important to both of you, how will it be useful in building your marriage?
4. If faith in Christ is not important to one or both of you, why do you wish a Christian ceremony, or a Christian environment for your nuptials?

4. Are there any skeletons in your closet?

Jesus answered, "Moses gave you permission to divorce your wives because you are so hard to teach. But it was not like that at the time of creation. I tell you, then, that any man who divorces his wife, even though she has not been unfaithful, commits adultery if he marries some other woman."
                                   (Matthew 19:8-9 GNB)

It is important to have in the open any issue that, if known, might create doubt about marriage between the prospective bride and groom. Experienced marriage and family counselors know there are one or more "skeletons in the closet" of most individuals' lives that can emerge to upset a marriage. Hidden experiences that could surface during the early years of your marriage should be resolved during the premarital period when you and the one you love are free to make decisions without compulsion.

Even religiously sophisticated persons have approached marriage with old poisonous experiences which must be drained of threat if the future is to be assured. Some serious problems that have emerged in counseling sessions but had never been shared with the partner include a former marriage, a child born out of wedlock, a drug history, a negative record with the police or the military, an intensive love affair or series of affairs, a medical record which would affect the relationship, and a record of unpaid bills. One couple experienced some serious tensions when the bride revealed after the wedding that she had undergone an abortion in high school, and the groom revealed he had been deeply in debt before he got married. That marriage was in trouble over matters which should have been resolved before the ceremony. Nothing had occurred after the marriage to threaten it, but threatened it was by undisclosed premarriage conduct.

Perhaps the most serious impediment to a prospective Christian marriage is a previous divorce. Often the divorced party believes the first marriage taught important lessons that will be applied to the second marriage. As a result, he may not wish to go through counseling at all, feeling it unneeded. Or he may be embarrassed to face questions related to his first marriage or the reasons for the divorce. Nearly 75 percent of divorced persons remarry. These marriages are less stable than first marriages. For some people divorce is repetitive. The problems that caused the divorce commonly follow into the second, third and fourth marriages. Later marriages often intensify earlier personality problems. The divorced partner is even less happy than he was in his first marriage. No professional counselor does his duty if he passes lightly over the divorce of one of his counselees.

It is true, of course, that many persons report happy second marriages. Most of these affirm that had they had the devotion and maturity in their first marriages they gave to the second, their first marriage would have been successful. Premarital counseling might have anticipated the problems that led to the divorce and prevented it from happening.

Christian men and women may respond to skeletons either more savagely or more sympathetically than they ought. If standards are not only high but so rigid that one partner will not forgive violations, there will be serious tensions. Some married Christians demand near-perfect behavior at all times. If they don't get it, they may find it difficult to relate to their spouses. If they are also distressed about serious lapses in their own conduct, imperfections in their spouse will be even more objectionable. Some women are repulsed by the thought of marriage to a divorced man, and some men cannot accept a woman who has experienced an abortion. Many men and women are put off by their partners' behavior, especially behavior relating to sexual intimacies that occurred before the offenders seriously thought about a lifetime relationship. One man came for counseling after his marriage because he had lost respect for his wife as a result of the excessive liberties she had permitted him before they were married. His own sense of responsibility for encouraging those liberties was not strong enough to enable him to forgive her. He apparently felt men could be freer than women.

One woman I was counseling about her marital problems became psychotic when she discovered that I had had cancer six years earlier. She was totally repulsed to be "in the same room with someone who had had that disease." Earlier she had told her husband that she could never live with him if he had a major illness. Her husband discovered that his wife had been well aware of her phobias before their marriage, but had concealed her problems because she feared he might reject her as his bride if she told him. When her problem emerged after marriage, he was deeply offended because her concealment suggested his wife questioned the quality of his love. Her fear of sharing her problems with him implied that she believed him to be a lesser man than he felt he was.

Impediments may not surface as marital problems for five, ten or twenty years after marriage. Many women who are pregnant at the time of their wedding will feel animosity toward their husbands for what happened. That animosity might not emerge until the child is in high school and becomes sexually active in the same way as his parents did fifteen or more years before. Women who became pregnant before they were married often experience guilt when their daughters reach puberty. They feel God is going to "get even" with them because of their sin, and judgment is presumed to be that the daughter will also become pregnant out of wedlock. The focus of the mother's fear often falls on her husband.

Sometimes dramatic experiences create impediments which may never be understood. One woman created constant tension with her husband, accusing him of lecherous interests in their daughter. The man, uncommonly patient, denied the accusations. Husband and wife told the same story—there were constant tensions over his alleged interests, but their own intimacy was gratifying to both, and both performed their duties in the family. In the course of counseling, the wife acknowledged that her father had often engaged in sexual activity with her. She feared her husband would conduct himself with their daughter as her father had with her. And there were other complications related to the wife's perceptions. One of the woman's secret reasons for marriage was to get away from her father, and to find a legitimate environment for sexual intimacy. Her father had aroused desire in her, and the guilt of her experience clouded her later relationship with her husband and daughter. The whole matter would likely have been exposed and treated in premarital counseling. If so, considerable unhappiness could have been avoided.

If any personal experience prior to marriage appears relevant to the future success of that marriage, it ought to be reviewed. It has already been suggested in this writing that whatever is resolved before the marriage produces a spirit of freedom, acceptance and forgiveness in a relationship. But it is equally true that unresolved issues can thoroughly poison a relationship until they are aired. However if a personal matter has been resolved, it should not be brought up.

FOR DISCUSSION:

1. Have you ever had a serious "love affair"?
2. Have you ever been engaged? Married?
3. Do you feel guilty or unable to talk about anything you did before you met the one you are now thinking of marrying?
4. How do you spend your private time together?
5. How long have you been engaged? What have you learned about each other during this time?
6. What circumstances would cause you to break your engagement?

5. What do you see as distinctive of a Christian marriage?

As the scripture says, "For this reason a man will leave his father and mother and unite with his wife, and the two will become one." There is a deep secret truth revealed in this scripture, which I understand as applying to Christ and the church. But it also applies to you: every husband must love his wife as himself, and every wife must respect her husband.
(Ephesians 5:31-33 GNB)

The greatest one among you must be your servant.
(Matthew 23:11 GNB)

Most of the young couples I have asked to describe a Christian marriage have said it is an intimate, loving relationship between a man and woman, or a means for meeting mutual needs. The responses were those which might well apply also to satisfactory secular marriages which possess no religious connotations. When this was pointed out, the counselees added virtues commonly identified with Christian perceptions, especially sacrificial love. Except for sexual intimacy, the feature recited could be provided by a father or mother, some other relative or friend. Very few couples, even with hints from the counselor, knew what was distinctive of a *Christian* marriage. To make it clear, I carefully review Ephesians 5:21-33 with the couple.

Christian marriage includes the traditional ideals which may be recited by anyone anticipating marriage, but it has a mysterious, dynamic and practical spiritual meaning as well. The husband should be the Christ figure in his family. Marriage becomes analogous to the relationship of Christ and the church. All that Christ would do for his disciples, or women, or children, or Christians in the church, a husband should do, insofar as he is able, for his family.

A wife is the church figure in the home. All that Christians in the church are to do for Jesus Christ and others, a woman is to do for her husband and children. As the church worships Christ, the wife respects her husband. As the church brings converts to spiritual birth and nurtures them, a wife gives birth to children and nurtures them. The Christian family is in this way and others a living analogy of Christ and the church. By it the Christian witness may be effectively transmitted. To violate the pattern will, to some degree, reduce the effectiveness of the family's Christian witness. Marriage may be broken through separation and divorce but it may be distorted, too, by failure to reflect its spiritual analogy. Persons who do not act like Christians warp the spiritual meaning of marriage, even though their marriages remain legally intact.

Many persons never think through the meaning of either the Christian faith or marriage because they are unwilling to work through the implications of either. The paradoxical parallels between them are numerous. Jesus, the Son of God, leader and greatest born of women, was a servant. His words fit his conduct: "He who is greatest among you shall be your servant (Matthew 23:11). The Christian is free, but "bound." He is not under law, but he is obedient to a life of purity and sacrifice. He shares the glory of Christ, but also the burden. Similarly in a Christian marriage, the husband is the head of the home, but he leads by serving. According to the Scriptures, he is to be the most loving, the most flexible, the most giving of the family members.

Headship is for the purpose of serving rather than being served. Headship will always emerge if two or more persons are involved. Someone speaks the last authoritative word, even in the most democratic of societies. Each person who leads must have taken or been given leadership. The Scriptures assign this leadership duty in the home to the husband. Submission to that leadership is the acknowledgement of wives that the husband's duty has been exercised, the order of Christ and the church has been confirmed.

Christian women today often admit that they dislike the implications of submission, unfortunately the most mentioned characteristic of the Christian wife. This submission reflects the submission of the church to Christ. It is not a subjection of women or a statement of inferiority to men. It must be voluntary and it is no more objectionable than the self-effacement and love requirements placed upon husbands. Submission is not childish obedience, and headship is not domination. And submission is not subjection. Subjection implies that a woman is unworthy or even less talented than her husband.

Arguments against the Christian view of husband and wife patterns cannot be logically constructed on the failures of many Christian marriages. Those marriages did not follow the pattern outlined by the Apostle Paul in Ephesians.

Nor can arguments be formulated from pagan views of leadership that place emphasis on self-aggrandizement, public career, money-making, fame or earthy conduct and life style. Despite all that Christian scholars do to focus on biblical order, the conduct of Christians often seems to be guided by the standards, interpretations and pleasures of the world at large, even to the interpretation of what may be done in and with families.

The teaching of Scripture is that marriage is a lifetime matter. It is supposed to be as permanent to natural life as the relationship between Christ and the church is permanent. Only by "hardness of heart" will mates force themselves to divorce each other. There are more than sufficient resources in the example of Christ, the fruit of the Holy Spirit, the Scriptures, prayer and spiritual living for any normal Christian couple to survive and prevail in marriage. To fail in a Christian marriage means failure somewhere along the line in the Christian lives of the mates.

Was it not the German Pietists and the early colonial Puritans that taught that the family was an *ecclesiola*, a "little church"? The emphasis of Ephesians 5:21-33 asserts a mystery, that of the church and Christ, but the mystery is partly understood in an appropriate Christian marriage, an *ecclesiola*. That is the essence of what is distinctive of a Christian marriage.

FOR DISCUSSION:
1. Can you differentiate the Christian view from other philosophies of marriage?
2. What do you see as the meaning of marriage?
3. Do you see marriage as a lifetime commitment?
4. What does or will headship and submission mean in your marriage?
5. Do you believe you have a spiritual gift for marriage (I Corinthians 7:7)?

QUESTION

6. What do you both know about your temperaments?

Please don't pay any attention to Nabal, that good-for-nothing! He is exactly what his name means—a fool!   (I Samuel 25:25 GNB)

Adequate preparation for marriage, once a careful choice of a prospective mate has been made, should also include: 1) adequate instruction about what marriage means, 2) a premarital conference and a physical checkup, and 3) personality tests and a program for adjustments suggested by a competent counselor.

It has already been suggested that some counselors have been fairly competent at predicting the success or failure of new marriages. The duration of a marriage is calculated by taking the lists of strengthening traits and dividing traits, and subtracting those that divide from those that strengthen it. The number of strengthening factors must exceed those that divide if a potential marriage is likely to be successful.

The idea of studying personality traits is not new. For centuries in many nations parental participation was vital to the mating of children, especially in the East. Marriage brokers in various parts of the world were remarkably successful in matching couples. They gave only minimal consideration to romantic love. Elements of fantasy and illusion, so influential today in selecting marriage partners in English-speaking countries, had little or nothing to do with their calculations. Modern psychological insights combined with the practical wisdom of parents and matchmakers should result in a larger percentage of successful modern marriages in the future. But young adults do not make enough use of available resources.

Marriage is not a destination: it is a journey. It must be able to face the wear and tear of daily existence. A flat tire, a minor repair, and even a breakdown now and then on that journey can be solved through adequate servicing. The vehicle need not be abandoned. And safe driving will avoid serious accidents. Every marriage needs safe drivers—knowing at least some of the errors to avoid, following standard rules, and knowing what to do in an emergency. Comfort on the marriage journey is gained in part by beginning with compatible company and becoming aware of the conditions to which one must adapt.

Many counselors insist that their premarriage counselees take the Taylor-Johnson Temperament Analysis Test. It is an excellent instrument that charts nine important affirmative traits and their opposites. They include: nervous/composed, depressive/lighthearted, active/social, quiet/expressive, responsive/inhibited, sympathetic/indifferent, subjective/ objective, dominant/submissive, hostile/tolerant, and self-disciplined/impulsive. Gradations are graphed on a standard form. The plotting includes self-perception and may also incorporate the perception of that self by a significant other. During the years that I have used the test it has proved its worth. Never has the administration of the test been a useless exercise.

Since the publication of *Spirit-Controlled Temperament* by Tim La Haye, the four well-known temperaments (the ancient Latins called them "humors") have been widely discussed. Although his review of the four temperaments—melancholic, sanguine, choleric, phlegmatic—and various combinations of them somewhat oversimplifies the matter, it is useful for laymen in the field of psychology. Discovery of one's own temperamental characteristics may be expected to help a person focus on issues related to marriage or other relationships in which he is involved.

It is well to review your temperament because opposites sometimes attract and tensions will result both before and after marriage. A choleric temperament combined with a melancholic temperament may appear both mysterious and exciting before marriage. Shortly after marriage the differences begin to create tension between the mates. What appeared attractive before union becomes irritating afterwards. Each wishes the other were more like he is. Similarity is yearned for.

If the marriage is to be happy, each mate must be open to the good aspects of the other person's temperament, and cope with the dark sides. In some marriages personality changes will assist in the development of acceptance. [23]

FOR DISCUSSION:
1. Whose temper, yours or your prospective mate's, is more volatile?
2. Who apologizes most readily when tensions are resolved?
3. Which of La Haye's four temperaments most fully describes your personality?
4. How do you handle hostility?
5. Has either of you ever been angered to the point of striking the other?

7. Why do you want to get married?

> Then the Lord God said, "It is not good for the man
> to live alone. I will make a suitable companion to
> help him." . . . . So the man named all the birds and
> all the animals; but not one of them was a suitable
> companion for him. . . . Then the man said, "At last,
> here is one of my own kind—Bone taken from my
> bone, and flesh from my flesh. 'Woman' is her name
> because she was taken out of man."
>   (Genesis 2:18, 20, 23 GNB)

The marriage rite which appeared in early editions of *The Book of Common Prayer* stated three basic reasons for marriage: the "procreation of children," "to avoid fornication," and "for the mutual society, help and comfort that one ought to have the other, both in prosperity and adversity."

These are ideals which were perceived out of Scripture and, to a large degree, represent social concerns and controls as well as individual happiness. When persons marry they are not likely to have thought about these issues. The first two statements are very proscribed, and the last large and general. If he breaks them down into their components, the Christian will find enough in the statements to begin his search for the meaning of marriage to society.

But most persons are concerned with personal arguments for marriage. They may or may not relate to the bearing of children, the avoidance of immorality or the ethical relationship to society. Even so, the reasons given for marriage in the *Book of Common Prayer* apply to a secular as well as a religious society.

Marriage satisfies four basic human needs: 1) the sex drive that draws two people together like an electrical charge; 2) the domestic urge that causes two persons to incorporate, to claim their own territory where they may establish a family unit under their own control; 3) the social need for companionship and status; and 4) a familial urge to generate, give birth, and rear one or more children. If these purposes are to be shared, they ought to be discussed by engaged couples so that misunderstandings may be avoided later.

One study showed that 45 percent of those who marry acknowledged that they sought marriage as the appropriate environment in which to satisfy their sexual drive. Sex was their primary motivation for getting married. Many couples, when asked their motivations for marriage, report that they are in love, wish to have some urge inside of themselves fulfilled in a marriage relationship, and feel they are "ready." As they experience different events at different stages in their lives—going to high school, getting a driver's license, getting a job—they feel it is now "time" to marry. Not to be married at age 25 or 26 is frightening for many people.

During the numerous premarital counseling sessions I have chaired in the course of a lengthy career, I have never been told by any individual, except at my prompting, that the reason why he or she wished to marry was to fully and intimately *serve the prospective mate*. But I believe each ought to believe and say, "This person above all other persons is going to be the object of my lifelong human service." After discussing this dynamic principle with a couple, I have often observed a visible change for the better in the persons before me who accept the idea. They understand, often for the first time, one of the most important purposes of marriage, though theoretically they should have known and believed it before the sessions began.

This intense desire to serve means that I, as a husband, will devote life and limb to my prospective wife; my salary check will be used to provide for her; my first wish will be for her comfort even if that creates some discomfort for me; my first defense will be of her, my first hope will be for her good, and if necessary I will forfeit my life to protect her life. No matter how idealistic and high-sounding this perception of marriage service may appear, many Christian husbands have realized it. I could cite many biographical events to prove the reality of that kind of ultimate devotion in many marriages. And I could also describe wifely commitments to the service of husbands. Her service, in her way, is like her husband's.

Marriage provides the context for the most complete and sacrificial service that one human being can give another. The traditional marriage vows infer this fact when they mention the extremes that may be encountered: sickness and health, poverty and wealth, love and obedience, and commitment to lifelong fidelity. If the prospective bride and groom can dedicate themselves to intense concern, total fidelity, complete sacrifice for each other before marriage, they will be freed from self-centeredness, and will open themselves to the possibilities of becoming the Christlike persons they are meant to become.

If my understanding of the nature of a good marriage is clear, I will want to choose the right person to become my wife. Her interests, feelings and needs will precede those of any other person who enters my life. I will give her my kindest words, my earnest empathy, my fullest forgiveness and my ablest comfort. I will do all that I can for her good. I will love her sacrificially.

Perhaps this total commitment may best be understood against the backdrop of marital failure. On several occasions I have counseled couples who have separated, or were on the verge of separation because the husbands had been deeply involved with other women with whom they had been intimate. The clandestine affairs had ended but the problems had not. Several husbands attempted to restore their marriages, but as the employers of the "other women" they could not bring themselves to terminate their employment. They protested that firing the women would be heartless, their suffering would be intense. They felt their wives should not insist that these employees, who had cost the family so much loss of family solidarity and peace of mind, be fired. The husbands were more willing to let their wives suffer than their former paramours. This strikes me as incongruous. It violates the principle of intense and total commitment to serve one's mate most fully under God.

There is another side to the issue. Not only do I wish to totally serve my partner, but I also wish to be totally served by her. We all have needs—physical, mental, emotional, social, spiritual. Each of these needs has elements which are exclusive. They are so private that no individual fully understands them as they relate even to his own life. If he marries he hopes to find a mate who will accept the mystery of his being, will not betray him and will reach deeply into his life to minister to his needs as only one person can do. It is his deep desire to meet his physical needs by eating, sleeping and sharing his body with this one person. He hopes to satisfy his spiritual needs by enjoying life with this one person and sharing his inmost thoughts. He wants to be comforted, accepted, loved, cherished to happiness by this one human being. He wishes to serve God through his spiritual identity with this mate who, believing with him, will pray in the same name, review the same Scriptures and talk the same language of faith. The Christian actually wishes to serve and be served totally in his marriage.

FOR DISCUSSION:
1. Do you wish to serve this person intimately and, insofar as you are able, refuse to permit anything except fidelity to God to interfere with that commitment?
2. What does this intense commitment and total fidelity in the development of your Christian life together mean to you?
3. Do you feel you understand the reasons for getting married better now than you did when you first started thinking about it?
4. In what ways do you think your prospective mate will suffer if you violate the principle of "mate primacy" discussed above?

8. Do you like each other?

That is why a man leaves his father and mother and is united with his wife, and they become one.
(Genesis 2:24 GNB)

A premarital counselor normally assumes that the prospective bride and groom love each other, even if an analysis makes their perceptions of love appear imperfect. The word "love" as it is commonly used in the English-speaking world has lost much of its significance. It has been cheapened, sentimentalized and distorted. Strident popular songs condition teen-agers to believe that love is a feeling one has or doesn't have, a feeling which happens magically. You presumably have little control over the feeling. Love is an accident. You *fall* in love.

But this is a far cry from the biblical view of love. The Scriptures affirm that love is a matter of the will. For that reason love can be commanded. All persons are commanded to love God. Jesus identified this commandment as the first and greatest of all commandments. Husbands are commanded to love their wives. Love is not something one waits for; it is something he makes happen. Unlike mere sexual attraction, real love is not based on good looks, competence, personality or other characteristics of one's mate. Biblical love is in the loving one, and may or may not be justified in the one loved. It is better to marry a loving person than to marry a person in love.

Love is vital to marriage, but it is a love (*agapé* in the Greek of the New Testament) which emanates from the will. It moves into the emotions, but does not have its roots there. Its motivations come from within the loving person. It is selfless, lasting and, like Christ's love, unearned. It is described in I Corinthians 13.

A number of unmarrieds were asked to grade a list of things they would like to have in marriage. Forty percent of the men put "companionship" in first place: only 15 percent put "love" first. Thirty-three percent of the women put "love" first: only 20 percent put "companionship" first.[24] Allowing for different perceptions and definitions, these differences between men and women are significant and should be discussed by prospective marrieds.

But love is not the concern of the question introducing this chapter. Do you really like each other? It is important to spend some time before you marry talking not only about *loving* but also about *liking*. Love may take on many burdens. As used in English-speaking countries, "love" is often a blinding emotion which for a period of time causes impaired judgment. Likes and dislikes are rather simple matters and provide practical focus for some issues. If you as a prospective bride say: "I love him, but sometimes I do not like him," the two of you can talk about loving and liking. What do you dislike in him? Will this become more serious later in your relationship?

You may tell yourself that he (she) will change or you will be able to change him (her). But don't forget the saying, "You cannot change the other person, you can only change yourself." Your partner's response will almost always be a defense of his behavior. When your mate tells you you aren't the person you ought to be, you instinctively defend yourself instead of thinking about whether to change. Instead of sharing, you have started to argue.

If a wife is chronically slow in being prepared to go out (negative), and her husband goes into a tirade (negative), this double failure increases the tension. The failure (negative) has produced a negative reaction, and the downward spiral begins. To meet lateness (negative) with patience (positive), with controlled communication (positive), with acceptance (positive) or some other positive approach, the prompt member may indeed produce a change in the tardy one. He will learn how to respond in ways that lead to an improvement in his responses even if his wife never overcomes her procrastination!

When you, as a prospective bride or groom, enter pre-marital counseling, you may already be at odds with your partner on numerous issues, most of which are probably minor but nevertheless potentially threatening. You may be spatting daily. If possible, several of your spats should be analyzed by a counselor. Generally you will be too embarrassed to acknowledge that you are already having difficulty. Be assured that nearly all couples at this stage in their relationships do disagree. As we have already pointed out, couples sometimes report that of all the periods in their relationship the engagement was least happy.

FOR DISCUSSION:
1. When did you last have an argument and what was it about?
2. How did you resolve it? Was it a satisfactory solution?
3. Do you honestly like (as well as love) your partner?
4. Do you think your marriage can be happy if your partner doesn't change?

QUESTION

9. What irritates you most in your partner's conduct?

> His wife said to him, "You are still as faithful as ever, aren't you? Why don't you curse God and die?"
> Job answered, "You are talking nonsense! When God sends us something good, we welcome it. How can we complain when he sends us trouble?" Even in all this suffering Job said nothing against God.
> (Job 2:9-10 GNB)

If you as a prospective bride and groom do not recognize in each other some irritating traits, you do not know each other well. In premarital counseling each person is generally reluctant to specify objectionable characteristics. If they do not come up with any, I remind them that the question will be repeated in ensuing sessions until they answer the question. You should know each other sufficiently well before marriage to recognize and openly acknowledge habits you don't like. On occasion the responses are both serious and humorous.

For example, one young woman complained about her future husband's habit of crossing his legs and bouncing his foot. She did not like this, was unsuccessful in persuading him to stop, and was doubtful that she could survive this and several other irritating habits. Assuring herself that she could change him, the young woman became his bride. In a short time they were at odds, and not long after they were divorced.

Another couple argued vigorously about the man's driving habits. His refusal to stay within the speed laws and his ferocity toward other drivers upset her. He did not change his habits even when she complained about motion sickness. He laughed at her concerns, and even exaggerated his unsatisfactory conduct when she protested.

Another woman complained about her fiancé's language. His use of "four-letter words" deeply offended her.

Still another bride-to-be was always correcting the grammar of her fiancé.

One woman was chronically upset by her husband's foreign accent. He found it difficult to improve his diction, and his wife was nervous whenever she heard him talk to anyone. Her nervousness, of course, made communications with others even more difficult for him.

All these women knew what their husbands were like before marriage. If before nuptials there were no adjustments, why would the women, accepting marriage with these men, not also accept their habits?

Numerous complaints about smoking or drinking also seem to be unrealistic and destructive. The spouse's habits were, after all, known before marriage. (Given my personal tastes, I would never permit myself to marry a person with such habits, but if I did I would hope I could treat that person fairly. If I married the person, surely I am implying at least minimal acceptance of his habits.)

That personal conduct is important, even in little ways, is demonstrated by the complaints registered in counseling sessions by troubled marrieds. One woman was distressed because her husband slept in his "underwear," another because her husband talked to himself, another because he pouted, another because he had a nervous laugh, another because he chewed his fingernails, and yet another because he would not read! The list seems endless.

Husbands complained that their wives did not dress up, did not fix their hair, did not use their time constructively, did not modulate their voices, did not put towels in the bathroom, did not close bureau drawers, did not plug in the telephone, did not clean house, did not put the top on the toothpaste, and did not brush dog hair from their clothes! This list could be as long as the women's complaints.

Both mates complained about smoking (men objected to bad breath, women to the health hazard), drinking (excessive drinking was not the only complaint; others included the bad example to children, the cost of the product and the tendency to press the non-drinking mate into the habit), driving (too fast and too reckless), language (crude, abusive and loud) and drugs (fear by the non-participating mate of the consequences of illegal use, fear for the safety of mate and children from the irrational behavior drugs cause). Drugs were also faulted by some husbands concerned about the well-being of the unborn children of their wives who were using narcotics. (Neo-natal addiction is common in infants.) Non-drug-using wives feared that insemination might be adversely affected by addicted husbands.

When other people are present, a Christian cannot act with complete freedom. The Bible expects him to act with sensitivity toward others. His conduct should benefit others. Most of the complaints made by premarriage counselees were reasonable, and future mates should have dropped or corrected their annoying habits. If a person cannot adjust for one he loves, he is not likely to adjust for "the weaker brother" (see I Corinthians 8-10).

Responsibility as well as sensitivity is important to mature persons and should influence husbands and wives to amend unsatisfactory conduct. The Scriptures give the Christian clear guidelines for a life style which promotes a healthy body and mind in which the Holy Spirit can most effectively achieve God's purpose for the person and his service for Christ. The ancient Latin aphorism, "A healthy mind in a healthy body," has never been improved on as an ideal.

But if your prospective mate is unwilling to shed an annoying habit, and you marry him nonetheless, you should stop nagging and protesting.

FOR DISCUSSION:
1. What things don't you like about your partner?
2. What habits distress you?
3. Are any of these habits likely to become more serious?
4. Can you live with your spouse-to-be if he does not change these habits?

QUESTION

10. Are you satisfied with your partner's manners?

Everything that happens in this world happens at the time God chooses.
> *He sets the time for birth and the time for death,*
> *the time for planting and the time for pulling up, . . .*
> *the time for making love and the time for not making love,*
> *the time for kissing and the time for not kissing.*   *(Ecclesiastes 3:1,2,5 GNB)*

"Lifestyle" does not refer only to the comforts you enjoy. It also refers to your value system. Much of your style of living reflects personal habits, peer pressures, conformity to the values of groups you belong to, and efforts to find yourself. "Accidents" and specific experiences of which you may be unaware also shape you. The clothing you wear, the way you wear it; the food you eat, the way you eat it; the car you drive, the way you drive it; the language you use, the way you talk—all these are factors that contribute to comfort or irritation for those around us.

During recent years the number of young wives who object to the attitudes and personal habits of their husbands has increased dramatically. The counter-culture's sometimes outlandish dress and crude language has offended much of the general society. Some young men expose more of their bodies than has been traditional by, for example, wearing vests without shirts. Their jeans are often faded, old and dirty, their hair unkempt. This neglect and casualness affects other things they do. For example, they may handle their food, and that of others, without first washing. Even in public places they pick up food with their hands, look at it, perhaps smell it, and return it to the serving bar.

In support of its belief in personal freedom and rights, society has tolerated considerable change in public conduct, not all of it for the better. Extreme casualness has brought down the level of human sophistication all along the line. Many young women suffer the loss in silence. But as they marry, their feelings often resurface.

The point is that future husbands and wives should discuss and resolve differences about their manners before they lead to unhappiness and argument. Ranges in social graces never seemed any greater than they were in the late 1960s. Or if they have always been great, they were never more irritating than during recent years.

One young woman, attractive and cultured, well groomed and competent with language, came for premarital counseling with her fiancé. He was a fine fellow with potential, but his lifestyle was completely different from hers. His hair was long and unkempt, his clothing casual at best, his shirt washed but unironed. I learned that when he ate he pulled his chair to the table, sat with his knees wide apart and his torso hunched over his plate. His arms moved like levers with the table as a fulcrum. He ate his meal without refinement. When she ate with him, she saw little more than the top of his head bowed over his plate.

And there were other features of their courting period which were as contradictory as their grooming, language and manners. He was monosyllabic, easygoing, unpunctual and apparently ignorant or unconcerned about those small courtesies which have characterized social conduct between men and women during recent centuries.

At first the young woman said the differences were not important to her. "Besides," she said, "I will help him change." Such a statement always raises warning flags for counselors. Marriage is not for the purpose of spouses changing each other. Changes will certainly occur, but not by manipulating or compelling a shift in the other. Many changes are totally unanticipated and unpredictable.

The man visibly bristled at her words. Perhaps he needed self-improvement, he acknowledged, but he felt the two should accept each other "just as we are." He felt that because he was willing to accept her refined ways she could accept his casual lifestyle.

I reminded the couple of several kinds of problems which had brought marrieds to counseling with me. One woman was distressed that her husband never attended to matters like waiting for her to get out of a car or go through a door. He made no effort to do anything "extra" on her behalf.

Another protested that she did not wish for her husband to hold doors for her or try to be chivalrous in any way. She interpreted the whole business of male manners with women as chauvinistic and implicit of an alleged weakness in women.

This feeling became sufficiently widespread in the 1970s that many men gave up trying to keep up the old traditions. As a counselor I was not judging either pattern, but the happiness of the prospective bride and groom depended on their agreement to accept each other's ways. I wasn't surprised when I later learned that the refined lady and her casual fiancé had broken up.

New husbands increasingly complain about the habits of their wives, too. They say that they are slovenly, spend too much time on their own interests and disregard the small amenities which make a man feel special to his wife. The most common complaint of all was that the wife was unappreciative. She acted as though her husband's loving acts were motivated by something other than love. That often destroyed her husband's motivation; he stopped sending flowers, buying gifts, taking her out, or making other intimate gestures.

Early in my own marriage I tried to express my affection for my wife by purchasing small gifts for her. I expected her to be excited and responsive. But more often than not, my gifts were not received appreciatively. My wife objected that the money could have been better used on some debt or saved for some other purpose. I almost reached the point of ending attempts at expressing my affection through small remembrances. Fewer were made. Nothing really changed in her attitude or mine. One day I purchased a dozen roses and was again criticized. I turned and left the room in a huff.

My wife's mother was in an adjoining room and heard the exchange between us. After I left she entered and talked with her daughter. (The conversation was later reported to me when my wife apologized for her remarks about the flowers.) Her mother said, "Your father tried to do little things for me, but I shut him off. We needed the money for something else, I claimed. He gave up. I would give anything if he were to bring a flower to me now. Don't end something you will regret you lost."

My wife accepted her mother's loving remarks. We have maintained these small gestures of our love and concern for each other through the years. When asked a few years ago by a friend if her husband had remembered her with a gift on a special day, my wife responded, "My husband doesn't seem to need a special event to get a gift for me." And I had forgotten to purchase anything on the day in question!

Some months after the death of comedian Jack Benny, his wife, Mary, was interviewed by the press. She responded graciously to questions about her personal life with Benny and her concern for her marriage to a man who could have easily, in the tinsel world of entertainment, broken fidelity with her. But at his death he had assured her of his love, and in his will provided a fund so that a florist would deliver a single rose to his wife each day of her life until her death.

QUESTIONS:
1. Do you like each other's manners?
2. Do you like each other's grooming and dress?
3. Do you plan to remember each other in small but special ways?
4. Do you have the same goals for your life together and for your marriage?
5. Do you have the same concept of beauty—in persons? in things? in nature?

QUESTION

11. Do you treat others better than your family members?

> *Do not speak harshly to a man older than yourself, but advise him as you would your own father; treat the younger men as brothers and older women as you would your mother. Always treat young women with propriety, as if they were sisters. . . . Anyone who does not look after his own relations, especially if they are living with him, has rejected the father and is worse than an unbeliever.* (I Timothy 5:1,2,8 JB)

During recent years much has been made of the need for sensitivity. But it seems as if we are less sensitive to each other now than before. A lot of talk does not assure greater sensitivity. I am appalled at the amount of sympathy demanded by some people who are unwilling to give it. Demanding voices make gentleness almost impossible, and prejudice makes sympathy extremely unlikely. Both seem to characterize this generation. It is difficult in such cases to raise conduct levels to reach our elevated theories about sensitivity and awareness.

One way to test genuine sensitivity between you and your prospective mate is to discover how you treat other members of your families. How do you treat your younger brothers and sisters? How do you interact with your parents? What household chores do you do? For example, who carries out the garbage? (If you no longer live at home, put all these questions in the past tense.)

If the answers are unsatisfactory, ask yourself why. If your mother carries out the garbage with four children at home, why? Are her children disobedient, insensitive or what? What tone of voice do each of you use with each parent? Is there constant bickering between parents and children? Do both parents demonstrate affection by hugging their children? Do you as the prospective bride and groom originate affectionate gestures with both parents? If only with one, why not the other?

Each prospective mate needs to ask himself, "Do you speak civilly to your friends and snap back answers to your parents? Would you do special things for non-family members and feel put-upon to do them for your family?" If you do not treat family members with sensitivity, no matter how greatly you protest the need for sensitivity, you cannot really expect it from anyone.

Your mother and father, until you leave home, provide many opportunities for the practice of sensitivity in a family. Their humanity, love, concern and even foibles give you opportunities for the expression of sensitivity. If adult children, on the eve of their marriage, are not sensitive to their parents, especially to that parent of the opposite sex, a prospective mate should see a possible danger signal.

Many premarriage couples acknowledged in counseling that they treated strangers better than family members, that it was the polite thing to do, and, for the most part, their parents had established the pattern they were now following. From numerous conversations it became clear that many parents were gracious to callers in their home, but raged when only family members were present. On occasion one or both parents turned chameleonlike within a matter of seconds when an unexpected visitor arrived at the door. These parent models established an inconsistent and hypocritical pattern of conduct for the children.

The principle of never treating another person better than your own mate is worth repeating. If you need to change your present behavior in this area, try asking yourself the following probing questions.

FOR DISCUSSION:
1. When was the last time you felt offended because your prospective mate seemed to show greater deference to someone other than you?
2. Is your feeling justified, or do you think you may be unduly sensitive or selfish?
3. Are you jealous or irritated when your partner is seen talking to a member of the opposite sex, and you are not occupied?
4. Are you able to practice patience with those you see most often?
5. Are you careful to make sure your beloved is cared for and comfortable before turning to your own interests?

QUESTION

12. How do you feel about your mother and father?

Jonathan said to David, "May the Lord God of Israel be our witness! At this time tomorrow and on the following day I will question my father. If

> *his attitude toward you is good, I will send you*
> *word. If he intends to harm you, may the Lord*
> *strike me dead if I don't let you know about it and*
> *get you safely away. May the Lord be with you as*
> *he was with my father!"*
>   *(1 Samuel 20:12-13 GNB)*

The relationship between a prospective bride and her father, and between a prospective groom and his mother, are instructive of the relationship which will develop between the groom and bride following their wedding.

Because a mother/son relationship is the most significant female/male relationship a man will have until marriage, its failure or success is suggestive of marriage success or failure. If the man expresses little tenderness for his mother, has not shown her physical affection, and has maintained a rebellious attitude toward her, he may experience difficulty in relating intimately to his wife. The matter is serious if he has treated his mother shabbily, rejected her advances of parental affection, and practiced a double standard of conduct (one in her presence and another away from home).

The mother may have contributed to the formation of negative attitudes by retreating from her son, showing no physical love, no instruction, no discipline, no identity. Whatever the cause of the problem, or whoever the persons at fault, the future of the marriage will be affected to some degree by unsatisfactory parent/child relationships.

The same thing may be said about the bride and father. If a daughter has experienced no physical affection, no visible signs of warmth from her father, she will probably have difficulty adjusting to the intimacies of marriage. A young woman who has not been embraced and kissed by her father and, most of all, has not felt appropriate affection from him as a male figure, may find sudden intimacy with her husband a traumatic experience that she may not happily resolve. That new relationship is total and intense. It is not fair to expect a woman to find the new experience easy when she has had no early appropriate tactile conduct to prepare the way for the larger experience.

If her father has never embraced her, held her hand, kissed her, she will likely recoil from the greater affection expressed in sexual intimacy with her husband. If the daughter is rebellious—harsh, unkind, selfish, aloof and disrespectful of her father—the husband-to-be should be warned by that attitude. A father/daughter relationship is highly prophetic of that of a husband and wife.

It is good for the prospective bride and groom to visit in each other's homes, get to know both sets of parents, and observe how the family home is managed as well as what happens between parents and children. A young woman engaged to be married was perceived to be mature, considerate and responsible. On a visit to her home her fiancé discovered she was spoiled, took advantage of her mother, spoke sharply and puckishly to her mother and father, and seemed to revert to her childish ways in the presence of her parents. The fiancé rightly concluded that the attitudes and conduct he observed would require discussion and resolution. This was done. The prospective bride quickly admitted in counseling that she took from others whatever she could by her system, but abandoned that system when it did not work. Her parents tolerated conduct which they should have corrected long before. The young groom confronted and dealt with the problems in good spirit from the outset of the marriage.

Ask yourself these questions: Is the mother a sloppy housekeeper? Do the mother and father fight? Are they effective parents with other children? Are they interested in life, education, work? Are they Christians? Nominal or dedicated?

Now ask yourself what your answers suggest about the future of your marriage. Even if your analysis is negative and you decide to get married anyway, knowledge of the problems to be confronted will make the effort worthwhile. On occasion this information has even saved a marriage.

FOR DISCUSSION:

1. What does your relationship with your parents suggest about your prospects for personal and sexual intimacy in your marriage?
2. Do you feel your parents are more affectionate to you than you are to them?
3. If you have been out of fellowship with your parents, has that fellowship been restored, and how was it done?
4. Are your mother and father affectionate to each other?
5. Are you like your mother or your father in your attitudes and actions? What implications does that have for your marriage?

QUESTION

13. How do you like your prospective in-laws?

Esau then understood that his father Isaac did not approve of Canaanite women. So he went to Ishmael son of Abraham and married his daughter Mahalath, who was the sister of Nebaioth. (Genesis 28:8-9 GNB)

Until engagement and marriage, a prospective bride and groom will likely feel their strongest individual loyalties to their own parents. Even with weakening family relationships today, people are concerned about their ties and roots. They may be at odds with their paternal families, but rise in defense of them when others are critical. And remember that nearly all other types of loyalties may be weaker than they were in former generations. In relative terms, family interests still hold a strong position.

As we have already stated, how you feel about your parents is one useful indicator of how good a marriage you are likely to have. A young woman who is deeply devoted to her parents will almost surely be unhappy married to a man who dislikes or holds little respect for them. In the early months of your marriage, there will be tense moments. You are likely to think and even talk about experiences you had at home before you were married. That very fact may aggravate the tension. Many young wives go "home" for a "visit" during at least one period early in marriage. They may not acknowledge their real purpose to either their husbands or their parents, perhaps not even to themselves. They are considering separation and, if permitted, will remain for weeks or months with their parents.

Acceptance of your in-law parents is more important, as a general rule, for a husband than for a wife. Young couples tend to visit the wife's home more often than the husband's. More attention should therefore be given to husband/in-law relationships. When, however, the husband does have a strong attachment to his parents, especially his mother, his wife may be expected to complain about the matter if she has to entertain her in-laws at meals on a regular basis, or share more of her husband's time than she wants to.

A husband, on the other hand usually accepts the fact that his wife will spend quite a bit of time with her mother. He may be particularly appreciative of that relationship if it affords him time for his own interests, or he perceives it as strengthening his wife in marriage. Obviously, the attitude of the wife's mother has much to do with the all-around acceptance of her by the son-in-law.

If the wife's parents are on good terms with their son-in-law, chances improve that the typical period of disillusionment after marriage will not destroy it. Understanding parents ought to try to effect reconciliation when breaks occur. This is not easy if they are dissatisfied with their daughter's choice for a husband. At this time the husband's attitude toward his wife's parents is vitally important. They don't want their daughter to return home. They don't want to be ready babysitters or surrogate parents. They don't want to see their adult child suffer through a marital ordeal, and, God forbid, return to childish ways. After all, adults don't run home to mommy.

Before the wedding every prospective groom should show an appropriate interest in his bride's parents. He should share his intentions with them. Young people believe, usually unjustly, that their parents should all of a sudden abandon all their concern for their children when they marry. They need to remember that their parents have invested years of emotion, money and planning in those children.

At the same time, of course, the bride and groom should be clear that their primary love and loyalty belong to each other. Their parents will not be around forever, and the new love and loyalty, hopefully established with the blessing of both sets of parents, will continue for some 25 or 30 years beyond the deaths of those parents. If for no other reason, the new marriage relationship is the more important one because the newlyweds will be around long after their parents are gone.

But, you ask, what about those couples who for some reason can't expect the approval of one or either set of parents? Differences in religion, goals, race and other factors may cause parents to be firmly opposed to a given marriage. Young couples will require careful counseling in such cases, and perhaps the parents will also need counseling. In any event, the matter of relationships between betrothed and parents cannot be disregarded. In most marriages the mates have not only married each other but also added a family on each side. That means three families are interlocked: the bride's, the groom's, and the new one which is born at the wedding. In-law problems appear second on the aggravation lists of many couples, right after disagreements about money, as a major cause of marital unhappiness.

It will be helpful to remember the following: 1) Never make a destructive comment to your mate about your in-laws; 2) Never accept a negative comment about your mate from your parents; 3) Never project the achievements of either of your parents upon your mate. Wives, don't talk about your father's ability to provide bountifully. Husbands, don't even mention your mother's superior cooking ability; and 4) Never underestimate the beauty of possible relationships with elder parents and other family members in the prayerful hope that your own children will regard you with consideration when roles are exchanged in the next generation.

FOR DISCUSSION:
1. Have you shared your wedding plans with both sets of parents?
2. Have you been kind to both sets of parents, even if one or even both have not been as supportive as you hoped they would be?
3. Do you see any problems in your relationships with your prospective in-laws that need to be discussed?
4. What, if anything, can you do to help each set of parents become friendly with the other?

QUESTION
14. Do you both have a sense of humor?

When people are happy, they smile, but when they are sad, they look depressed.
(Proverbs 15:13 GNB)
Is anyone among you in trouble? He should pray. Is anyone happy? He should sing praises.
(James 5:13 GNB)

As a counselor who has worked with both happy and unhappy marriages, I am convinced that too little recognition has been given to humor as a vital factor in a stable marriage. Happy couples not only enjoy humor, but they can laugh and joke with each other.

A good sense of humor is also crucial to little children. Some children report that they don't ever remember seeing or hearing their parents laugh. Too many homes are solemn to the point of gravity. No wonder there's a generation gap! The older generation may look upon easy humor as evidence of shallowness, or even spiritual immaturity. The younger generation may presume that humor is a reflection of truth and good will.

Sometimes a counselor can see how serious a marital problem is by observing how the husband or wife responds when a humorous idea is injected into conversation. People who are angry at each other won't laugh. They feel deep down inside that a smile or a laugh would imply approval, and they don't want to give even that much encouragement to someone else. This hostility may also be seen in exchanges between heads of state or parliamentary opponents. When humor occurs in such cases, it is usually cutting and derogatory. Humor can, in fact, be one of the most malicious forms of speech.

Many humorous remarks focus on family members and situations. Situation comedies usually poke fun at family foibles. Wife jokes are presumed to be particularly hilarious. Some liberationists have protested both wife and women jokes because they see them as denigrating to women. Other people have introduced jokes about men, and husbands specifically, but, some argue, they do not seem to be as funny as jests about women.

But for many years television has offered the public several shows in which the husband and father was a bumbling dolt. The popularity of these shows suggests that people will laugh at men in comical situations as readily as they will at women. Women comics (increasing in number) tend to concentrate on men and husband jokes, men comics on women and wives. Both utilize personal derogation to get a laugh.

If one of the partners in a marriage is humorless, the couple should talk it over in premarital counseling. The easygoing or glib member must become aware that his humor will sometimes be taken seriously, and on occasion embellished beyond all logic by his mate.

And most people, even those who enjoy a good laugh,

have limits. If the exchange is extended for any length of time, we begin to feel that the humor may be barbed. Or we weary of the game. We feel it's time to get back to serious conversation. The joking mate needs to be able to detect those times when horseplay, jesting, or just plain lightheartedness has gone on long enough.

Most marriages, however, are probably afflicted with too little humor, not too much.

FOR DISCUSSION:
1. Do you enjoy a good joke when you are with your friends?
2. Would you describe yourself as a person with a good sense of humor?
3. Do you feel you and your prospective mate are compatible on matters of humor?
4. Do you think your sense of humor will help make your marriage successful?
5. Do you feel you can tell a funny story?
6. Do you often use "humor" as a weapon?

QUESTION

15. Are you easily offended?

> *Then Sarai said to Abram, "It's your fault that Hagar despises me. I myself gave her to you, and ever since she found out that she was pregnant, she has despised me. May the Lord judge which of us is right, you or me!"* (Genesis 16:5 GNB)

A team of University of Michigan researchers reported that during the first two years of marriage "52 percent of American wives are reasonably well satisfied with their husbands, but 20 years later only six percent are well satisfied and 21 percent are conspicuously dissatisfied."[25] A lot of this unhappiness should not be present if persons are sufficiently accepting, mature and loving. Much of what has been written and said since then implies that husbands and wives are even less satisfied now than they were 20 years ago.

Interpersonal relationships, like marriage, are often weakened by the common human tendency to be easily offended. Persons believe themselves to be victimized in many situations, and if one feels victimized he is offended. Even so, most offenses are self-inflicted. Most of us do not deliberately try to offend other people. We often twist other people's words to mean what was not intended. We assume that the other person is trying to hurt us when nothing could have been farther from his mind. We would be appalled to discover that they sometimes feel we are trying to hurt them! They have no evidence, we say, for that opinion of us. But we have none for our presumed beliefs about their attitudes, either. All of us are victimized by our own humanity, by our almost irresistible assumption that the words and conduct of others are loaded and malicious. We don't usually presume people are innocent until proven guilty.

People everywhere seem unduly sensitive about how they will be treated. Much of this fear is accounted for by their lack of self-esteem, insufficient knowledge about the human condition and an oversupply of basic suspicion about the motives of others. For reasons not fully clear, these evils are especially noticeable when people get married. Not only does a husband or wife become edgy about the words, gestures, omissions and acts of his or her partner, but the children for the same reasons question the sincerity and love of their parents and their interest in them. Each child in a multi-child family believes on occasion he is least liked or appreciated among the children. All the remaining children are better treated and get more than he does. Unfortunately, parents permit a self-pity to remain and grow until it is no longer simply a childish reaction but a cause for prolonged suffering in later experience.

Because the survival of a child and happiness seem to turn on his ability to cling to pieces of self-pride, or on his skill in blaming others for his problems, he becomes guilty of pride and defensiveness. He blames or is suspicious of others. And the world is large enough for most clever persons to get away with this technique and survive. They can make new friends to replace offended or offensive ones, or move to a different location to start afresh or take a new job. At last they die and the fruitless competition is ended.

But in a good marriage you have to face these matters. One day, early or later in marriage, your husband or wife may call a halt to the pattern. There is no escape or rationalization. The husband or wife may refuse to be made the scapegoat any longer. The accusations and the blame must be dealt with or the marriage will be lost in sullen silence, bitter wrangling, perhaps even separation or divorce. Even if the marriage remains legally intact, if it is unhappy it is in many ways lost.

Early in a marriage a bride may be sensitive to any slight. She is troubled by her own insufficient self-esteem (a lifelong concern) and intoxicated by a headiness over her new status. Then the real humdrum of life starts and she yearns to hold on to the romantic level of the first weeks of marriage which seems to be subsiding as routine asserts its demands. Her husband phones in the afternoon. An overtime assignment will delay him and dissolve their plans to eat out that evening. So she speculates. He has broken his promise. He is working too much. Other people are receiving priority.

The pyramid of pressure is beginning to build. As it builds, the mortar of imagination bonds the blocks of real or alleged evidences together to make a case for accusation. The need for marriage counseling is obvious. Yet it is not likely to be sought. Matters will worsen. The young wife may go to her mother for a "visit." Perhaps one of the mates will walk away from the marriage.

Relevant questions and ideas help a couple discover reality. What is the point of offending an acquaintance, or a mate, or a child? Why would a person, in his right mind, wish to deliberately hurt another? At the beginning of a relationship the best in people is easily brought out through trust, communication, humility, objectivity, sensitivity. But when a person's good intentions and attitudes are met with doubt, suspicion and accusation, there is hurt. People who are hurt often inflict injury, usually of the same kind that wounded them, and deterioration of a relationship is under way. Being aware that this is a common occurrence in marriage is an important factor for alleviating misunderstanding and preventing tragedy.

FOR DISCUSSION:
1. How easily are your feelings hurt?
2. Do you believe that there will be a marriage problem because of any low tolerance levels you permit?
3. Do you feel sufficiently threatened in stress situations to use fallacious arguments to justify yourself?
4. How often have you deliberately tried to hurt another person?
5. What steps can be taken by either of you to avoid hurt feelings?

QUESTION

16. What is your attitude about your wife working outside the home?

How hard it is to find a capable wife! She is worth far more than jewels! . . . . She looks at land and buys it, and with money she has earned she plants a vineyard. . . . She makes clothes and belts and sells them to merchants. . . . She is always busy and looks after her family's needs.   (Proverbs 31:10,16,24,27 GNB)

A century ago women made up 15 percent of the wage earners. In 1977 they made up between 40 and 45 percent of the work force. Some women do not wish to work outside their homes, but feel compelled to do so because of family needs or expectations which cannot be met by one salary. Other women are out of work and cannot find jobs. Still others cannot get an outside job because they have to take care of small children. Many women with preschool children work because they are the only support for their broken families. Other women, free to work if they wish, do not choose to do so. Even so, the basic fact is that women make up nearly half of the labor force. National and state laws force employers to reconsider hiring policies. These compel the consideration of women at every job level.

Although a high percentage of women workers are young, many older women now work. Increased longevity—considerably beyond childbearing years—and the ease with which a home may be maintained make it possible for older women to develop outside interests. And because the use of their time is amply rewarded with money, women feel their worth is increased through entrance into the job market. However, the benefits are mixed with disadvantages.

In general, working women who are energetic appear less anxious or depressed than their homebound sisters. Many seem less resentful of their husbands, even expressing romantic interests more fervently than full-time housewives. A larger percentage of homebound wives become alcoholic and suicidal. They profess boredom with their lives and duties. They are ambivalent about what they do as housewives, alternately defending their worth and putting themselves down.

Women who work outside the home are more likely than full-time housewives to become independent from their husbands, more likely to become romantically interested in other men, and more likely to neglect domestic chores in their homes. Those who lose the most, however, are the children of mothers who work outside the home. Law enforcement officers generally expect youths in trouble to come from families in which the mother has a full-time job away from the family. Urie Bronfenbrenner stated the point clearly:

> Increasing numbers of children are coming home to empty houses. If there's any reliable predictor of trouble, it probably begins with

children coming home to an empty house,
whether the problem is reading difficulties,
truancy, dropping out, drug addiction, or
childhood depression.[26]

In all, the dangers of one approach appear to be matched
by those of the other. Dependent children appear to be the
main concern of the wife when she decides whether to stay
home or enter the labor force. There is nothing in the Scriptures which demands one or the other for Christian women,
if the personal needs of the family are met. Rearing children
is the duty of both parents, but the mother must be willing to
sacrifice her external interests if the needs of the children
collide with them, and her husband is unwilling or unable to
meet related domestic requirements.

The Scriptures are firm about order. Order is vital to the
tranquility of society, and especially required by the personal
needs of children. To assure order in the family, roles for
father, mother and children have been designed. Christian
parents who fulfill their respective roles seem to be satisfied
with them.

It is likely that God accepts different patterns as long as
they protect children, strengthen love bonds and develop
spiritual and social life. His plan, which places primacy of
domesticity upon women (if they are married) and primacy
of breadwinning upon men, resolves conflicts. Where parents can agree on sharing chores, disciplining and nurturing children, organizing family life and meeting the needs of
family members, there is no biblical reason why father and
mother may not work outside their home.

Family counselors discover differing attitudes between
mates about working wives. Many wives do not wish to
work or develop a career either for salary or status. As a
matter of fact, some women acknowledge that they marry so
they will not have to work outside the home. If this motivation is strong and a marriage is constructed on little more
than laziness or self-interest, trouble rises early for the
couple. The motivation is not sufficient to build a gratifying

marriage relationship, even if the wife is domestically inclined. Commonly, the wife who marries to escape the competition and prescription of an outside job is also a poor
housekeeper.

Many husbands insist that their wives find jobs. Perhaps
there are more husbands who expect their reluctant wives to
assist in the breadwinning than there are those who resent
their wives working. Counselors see more wives who are
intimidated into working than those who are prevented
from doing so. In these instances some wives complain that
their husbands encourage them to take outside jobs, but do
not share domestic duties in the home. The complaint is
justified.

Before marriage, the prospective bride and groom ought
to settle on work policy, especially for the period of child-
rearing. This problem was alluded to earlier in this discussion. It is clear that children have not been sufficiently regarded by society. About three of four mothers with children
aged six to seventeen work outside their homes. One of six
children is reared by a single parent, and most single parents
have jobs. More than half have preschool children. All these
make for "high risk" families.[27] Analysts are left to conclude
that many women who could work because they have no
dependent children do not work. And many women who
should not be in the work force because they have dependent children are working.

According to the eminent report, *Toward a National Policy
for Children and Families*, every child under the age of six
requires the constant care of an adult. Although day-care
centers and other institutions may be useful and necessary
for temporary services such as helping families meet
emergencies, no adequate substitute has yet been found for
mother or father figures in nurturing children. As society is
presently constituted in the United States and Canada, children need their own home and identity.

Couples should resolve potential problems in favor of the
children they bear. When children are not involved, the

issues should be confronted and resolved in a spirit of equality and good will. There is room for flexibility. No one pattern is dictated.

FOR DISCUSSION:
1. Is the wife willing to give up temporarily her own professional goals for the sake of her children?
2. Is the husband willing to give up some of his own interests in order to be an effective parent to his children?
3. Do bride and groom agree on occupational and home care duties and privileges for both husband and wife?
4. Do bride and groom acknowledge that they will change, even in a matter like occupational interests, as their marriage matures, and that adaptations will be appropriate to accommodate those changes?

QUESTION

17. Do you believe anyone should help you financially?

I am not saying this because I feel neglected, for I have learned to be satisfied with what I have. I know what it is to be in need and what it is to have more than enough. I have learned this secret, so that anywhere, at any time, I am content, whether I am full or hungry, whether I have too much or too little.
(Philippians 4:11-12 GNB)

Church helpers should hold to the revealed truth of the faith with a clear conscience. They should be tested first, they are to serve. We did this, not because we do not have the right to demand our support; we did it to be an example for you to follow. While we were with you, we used to tell you, "Whoever refuses to work is not allowed to eat."   *(2 Thessalonians 3:9-10 GNB)*

Does financial assistance from parents create negative effects on married children? Does it affect the parents? McCall's magazine surveyed 84 young married couples who were examples of a new kind of young family, held together with some love, a government loan, a college scholarship, a small apartment, and a monthly check from the parents. When asked if parental help created bothersome psychological problems, six out of seven respondents said that it did.[28]

The question arises naturally, "Is there ever a time when parents should assist their married children?" By and large, assistance has been common throughout most historical periods. Children were given a corner of the farm, a job with father in the local store or dowries. Those children succeeded to farm ownership or partnership and the cycle was complete, only to be begun again for the next generation. In modern times gifts of money, sometimes desperately needed by newlyweds, are not generally related to their labor for the paternal family or their assumption of duty to those parents. The opportunity for sibling service is not present as it was in rural society. The current problem of launching youth into adult life is more complex. With appropriate planning, review, goal setting and adaptation to each situation, effective solutions to this knotty problem can be found.

Nearly all counselors contend that when parents assist their adult children, especially married ones, the assistance should relate to a particular project, with a mutually agreeable termination date. If a goal is set which is agreeable to parents and children the goal itself becomes the focus. If additional education is desired by the young couple, the parents may contribute to the completion of a course of study projected over a specified period of time. The success or failure of the couple to reach the goal might well determine if any future assistance will be proffered. In any event, each agreement is closed and any new ones rest on their own merit. No "I told you so" or "I would have done it another way" should interfere with the relationships between parents and their adult children.

To keep harmony in the family, parents should review their motives in giving their children money. Are they deliberately delaying the maturation process to make their children continually dependent? If so, there may be a parental ego problem which takes advantage of the children's straightened circumstances. If the parents desire to make up for earlier tensions or seek an inordinate return of gratitude, the gift may create more problems than it will solve. Young couples who receive assistance may not be able to return enough gratitude to satisfy their parents.

One's adult children must be set free to make their own way. The chains of money are fearfully forged. If gifts of money are not just that—they should be refused. The temporary loss to the couple will be minor compared to the loss of personhood, maturation, integrity, freedom and self-respect. Whatever strings are attached must be mutual ones, holding value for both the giver and the receiver.

FOR DISCUSSION:
1. Are there any financial bonds between either of you and any family members which might affect your marriage?
2. Do you feel free to share with your parents the issues which relate to their involvement in the marriage?
3. Are you as independent about financial matters as you are about your other personal affairs?

QUESTION

18. What is your plan for budgeting?

As the scripture says, "The one who gathered much did not have too much, and the one who gathered little did not have too little." . . . Our purpose is to do what is right, not only in the sight of the Lord, but also in the sight of man.
					(2 Corinthians 8:15,21 GNB)

There are several common forms of budgeting used by families. The most simple is a bank deposit system. A couple deposits all income into a checking account and makes out checks for all necessities, living on the residue. If the residue is insufficient, the cost of necessities is adjusted by reducing the family's lifestyle. For many marriages the system works well enough because it is kept simple and the expectations of the members of the family are never permitted to exceed available funds.

People who are more sophisticated in money management will generally find this simple pattern unsatisfactory. They see a checking account system as little more than a stop gap, and sense the importance of planning for the future.

A common system of formal budgeting is based on percentage calculations. As noted elsewhere in this series of questions, money percentages are related to values. One family prizes a fine home; another prefers to have a more modest home and buy a camping trailer as well. The formula must be kept exactly at 100 percent on both income and outgo. If there is excess in the income it is held (savings) or dispersed (prepayment) according to prearrangement so that income and expenditures total the same amounts for book balancing. The excess may be credited to savings or anything the couple feels will justify the assignment of surplus. Percentage assignments appear ideal for nearly all income levels. For example, a family may determine to spend no more than 25 percent of its income on food, no matter how much the income may be.

Even children may be taught money management by dividing their smallest allowances into predetermined accounts. Our children used the 10-80-10 schedule of their parents from the time they were small. They gave ten percent to the church and saved ten percent. They "lived" on 80 percent, using it for such things as toys, clothes, Christmas gifts or vacation spending money. All excess was put into individual education accounts.

Small ledger books are available from stationery stores.

With minimal instruction, a person can develop skill in using the columnar system for recording income and expenditures. At first the bookkeeper should be very specific about items, such as 25 cents for a writing pen. Later, as the couple prove their ability to live within a budget, the expenditures may be grouped so that a pen would be paid for out of the allowance for incidentals or personals.

Early in our marriage, during college years, my wife maintained a very simple but effective system. She bought a set of small yellow cans, each slotted to receive coins or paper money. She divided our income into the boxes according to formula. I recall that $3.00 went into the "meat" can (World War II was in progress). She would also put notes into the cans to guide her on necessities to be purchased before anything else in the category could be bought or the money transferred to some other can. The plan worked very well, and got us through college with a baby, and later a second child.

It should be understood that changes in society will force changes in budgets. For example, housing costs increased between 1950 and 1976 to take nearly four percent more of the family's income. (Housing costs increased dramatically, but salaries also increased so the percent of a family's paycheck that went to pay the mortgage did not rise as drastically.) Utilities took nearly two percent more from a paycheck in 1976 than they did a quarter of a century earlier. Health costs leaped from 4.7 percent of a paycheck in 1950 to 7.4 percent in 1976. With dramatic rises like these something had to be reduced. Clothing expenditures dropped from 11.7 percent of a paycheck in 1950 to 7.4 percent in 1976. Percentages used for food declined from 28.1 percent to 20.4 percent. Home upkeep (not including utilities) decreased. Transportation and recreation shares of income did not change significantly during the 25 years.[29] With changes taking place, sometimes annually, no standard budget formula can or ought to be recommended.

An intriguing feature of budgeting is that it is fun once a

couple establish a pattern of budgeting. The game is worth playing, with each couple winning. Budgets make persons future-oriented. Rather than paying only for what is past, a couple can create for a future. Anticipation is an important factor in happiness, sometimes more meaningful than realization. What dream is not larger than reality? Living for future experiences offers a sense of freedom, of control of one's destiny. And, if nothing else, a well-designed plan saves the high cost of servicing debts and paying interest.

FOR DISCUSSION:
1. Are you willing to develop a plan for spending and stick to its requirements?
2. Are you willing to amend the plan as situations change?
3. Are you willing to change your lifestyle as a means for balancing your budget?
4. Are you willing to delay some of your most intense acquisitional desires to gain balance in the family budget?

QUESTION
19. Are you going to share your incomes?

Well, religion does make a person very rich, if he is satisfied with what he has. What did we bring into the world? Nothing! What can we take out of the world? Nothing! So then, if we have food and clothes, that should be enough for us. But those who want to get rich fall into temptation and are caught in the trap of many foolish and harmful desires, which pull them down to ruin and destruction. For the love of money is a source of all kinds of evil. Some have been so eager to have it that they have wandered away from the faith and have broken their hearts with many sorrows.   (1 Timothy 6:6-10 GNB)

During the first part of the 20th century it was fashionable for many wives who worked to retain their earnings for them-

selves. The positive image of a husband was in direct proportion to his ability to provide for his family without assistance from anyone. Working women were not highly paid
and they, even though married, often used their money for
"extras"—like clothes, gifts, furniture, or savings. Married
women perceived their work as a way to create luxury. As
times changed, women worked in greater numbers, made
more money and were improved in status. World War II
beckoned them to factories and two-salary families became
commonplace.

Many double-salaried families encountered serious
problems in accepting traditional roles for husband and
wife, in caring for dependent children, and in working out
the responsibilities of the home. Among the problems they
had to solve was the division and control of their income.
Different formulas were worked out. Some wives insisted
on keeping all they earned and did not feel they were obligated to tell their husbands what they did with their pay-
checks. Some wives refused to lend money they earned to
their husbands to meet some emergency, such as house
repairs. Even today some women maintain this standard.

In some marriages the wife speaks of *our* money (that
which the husband earns), and *my* money (that which she
earns). And some men hold the "hers" and "mine" perception of money and things. Marriages built on this dichotomy
often appear forlorn and unhappy. There are some situations in which this independent arrangement may be satisfactory for happiness, but they usually occur in families
which are affluent.

Working husbands and wives sometimes put equal
amounts into an account to pay all expenses. Whatever is left
over can be used as they please. In one instance, the couple
divided an inheritance into equal parts so that each mate
could do as he pleased with his share. A similar arrangement
seems attractive for many couples, but for others it intimates
either distrust or inability to talk out goals. One couple

divided resources so that the husband could invest in the stock market, something his wife feared to do. She protected her portion through bank deposits. They were pleased with the arrangement. It helped rather than hindered their marriage.

Solidarity in a family is often reflected in the way money is valued. If, without reason, money is kept out of the hands of one's mate, then the importance of the mate is minimized and that of money is overemphasized. If there is no personal weakness which requires that resources be protected from dissipation by one spouse, money should be treated as a tool useful to both family members.

Mutual trust assigns money its place with neither too much nor too little attention. It is to be managed for the good of all. It is not to be loved nor despised. Used in the biblical sense, money should be handled humbly for things that bring enjoyment, should be dedicated for God's purposes (through good works and sharing), and be explained through social application, with all related to spiritual benefit (1 Timothy 6:17-19).

Any plan for efficient money management which is agreeable to the husband and wife, and makes them good stewards as well as happy, must be approved. But this assumption is based on each partner knowing how the other feels about money matters. It is presumed here that that information should be shared when required by either mate. It is significant that disagreement over money management is directly related to the failure of one mate to communicate with the other about earning or spending. The assumption holds that unless there is an amicable division of income between mates all major funds should be mutually controlled.

"Sharing bed and board" is an old aphorism. All things being equal, the "one flesh" principle should also hold for ownership of property, of which money is the easiest to handle and negotiate.

FOR DISCUSSION:
1. Are you going to pool financial incomes?
2. Are you agreed on any special division of a portion of the family income?
3. Are there national or state laws which provide special benefits for separating or uniting accounts?

QUESTION
20. Who will balance the checkbook?

> *And God is able to give you more than you need,*
> *so that you will always have all you need for*
> *yourselves and more than enough for every good*
> *cause. As the scripture says, "He gives*
> *generously to the needy; his kindness lasts*
> *forever." And God, who supplies seed for the*
> *sower and bread to eat, will also supply you with*
> *all the seed you need and will make it grow and*
> *produce a rich harvest from your generosity. He*
> *will always make you rich enough to be generous*
> *at all times, so that many will thank God for*
> *your gifts which they receive from us.*
> *(2 Corinthians 9:8—11 GNB)*

In a poll of American women more than 55 percent said that money caused most of their arguments with their husbands. Raising children was named by 16 percent, and confronting in-laws was stipulated by 10 percent.[30]

Clearly, in this poll, money problems irritated more than three times as many wives as the second aggravation. Joseph B. Trainer of the University of Oregon Medical School supported the primacy of money as a problem-maker when he stated: "In marriages where there is conflict, 85 percent of the time it is based on money problems. Even in happy marriages, 45 percent of the conflicts are based on money differences."[31] It is important, then, to reduce fiscal problems which cause so much tension in marriage.

The most helpful answer to the question, "Who will

balance the checkbook?" is, "The one who manages it best."
A poll showed that 57 out of 100 homes were managed
fiscally by the wife, 24 by the husband, and 19 by both
husband and wife.[32]

There is no aura of authority which pertains to balancing
books. Money should not be afforded the importance which
some husbands give it when they relate their own primary
authority to managing family funds. The treasurer need not
be, and seldom is, the head of a corporation. Jesus did not
manage offerings. The apostle Paul referred money matters
to laymen. The early church elected deacons in order not to
distract their leaders.

Persons tend to be either spenders or savers. A spender
spouse is likely going to wreak havoc with his family. Unfortunately, however, the more frugal partner tends to let the
spender take control of the family budget. Otherwise arguments over the use of credit cards, to cite just one example,
frequently threaten to break up the marriage. Education
assists uncontrolled spenders if they are willing to submit to
discipline.

It would have been far better, of course, had financial
education taken place during a person's formative years.
Youngsters, given money, quickly reveal their tendencies
one way or the other: spenders or savers. (We had, among
our four children, two of each.) When parents discover the
tendency of the child, education for money management
ought to begin. Both tendencies introduce problems, but the
spenders will cause more family grief by far than the savers.

As already noted in an earlier passage, management of
family income should be guided by a budget. This is a plan
determined by the value systems of a couple, and implemented through careful self-discipline. No single budget
plan will suit all families. With variant values, interests,
children and communities, different budgets will appear for
different families.

Even so, there are basic precepts which may be applied
across the board for nearly all families:

a. Resist urges to include in spending plans any special income—bonuses, overtime or such windfalls as gifts from affluent family members. Emergencies may be expected to absorb unscheduled or unanticipated income.

b. Resist fantasies about any social or lifestyle levels which one believes he ought to have or wishes he had that he cannot afford. Choose a realistic level that a standard family income can support. Especially should one choose a home appropriate to his earning range.

c. Resist tendencies to use up all resources. This means that savings should be treated as an indebtedness to oneself. Save 10 percent of your income.

d. Resist temptations to avoid giving. Give away 10 percent for the purpose of Christian mission. People who do not give do not follow the life and ministry of Christ. And they deny a basic human need to help others.

e. Resist the suggestion to live on more than 80 percent of standard net income. Except for necessities, do not buy anything new until all debts are current. When one's entire paycheck is fully committed by debts before it is received the planning has been poorly done. If the budget has no flexibility it could suggest that one is not in control of his affairs.

FOR DISCUSSION:
1. What can you do to avoid tensions over money matters in your marriage?
2. Will the person balancing accounts be willing to respond graciously to the inquiries of the other?
3. Is one a spender and the other a saver, or do both belong in the same category?

QUESTION

21. Have you discussed giving to worthy causes?

Give to everyone who asks you for something, and when someone takes what is yours, do not ask for it back.   *(Luke 6:30 GNB)*

> *If you take someone's cloak as a pledge that he will*
> *pay you, you must give it back to him before the*
> *sun sets, because it is the only covering he has to*
> *keep him warm. What else can he sleep in? When*
> *he cries out to me for help, I will answer him*
> *because I am merciful.   (Exodus 22:26-27 GNB)*

How you spend your money may be a better barometer of
your values and perceptions of the meaning of money than
what you save or give. Some people reveal their self-centeredness and lack of love by the complete absence from
their budget of all charitable causes. But other people are
generous to any friends who request assistance. The purposes, good or ill, of those friends had little to do with the
generosity of the givers. They are indiscriminately generous
to everyone—except their wives! The wives are limited in
their spending and receive no benefit from their husbands'
largesse to others.

One man enjoyed taking friends to lunch. He readily
picked up the check and was pleased to do so. But he
questioned any indulgence in gracious living by his wife.
She could not, without creating family tension, take her
friends to lunch or "waste" even a small amount on some
bauble. They not surprisingly wound up in a marriage counselor's office.

Although extravagance is a major problem in an untold
number of marriages, penury is a problem in others. And too
often the person responsible for this problem is the man. His
feelings about money are generally forced as absolutes on
his family. No questions may be raised. Some wives are
compelled to buy the lowest priced products; her worth is
based on her ability to manage her family at near poverty
levels. The whole matter is spiritualized and cast in religious
terms relating to sacrifice. The man's dedication and sacrifice
may even mean greater giving to Christian organizations.
But if there is no agreement between husband and wife, the
sacrifice is not a complete virtue.

Some people are conditioned to limit their business,

recreation and family activity and even the work of Christ because of a distorted belief in money as a special and even sacred thing. They sacrifice time, efficiency, and relationships to save a few dollars. They watch for uncanceled stamps on envelopes, take advantage of the smallest store sale, and borrow items when they should buy them. They are drudges—on their way to becoming misers—and don't realize it. Unless their mates can adapt themselves to this stinginess, there will be considerable unhappiness.

FOR DISCUSSION:
1. Do both husband and wife have equal privileges of using casual funds?
2. May every member of the family, including children, have a personal savings account for his own purposes?
3. Is it understood that God is able to provide abundantly?
4. Is it understood that money is a tool that may be used skillfully or clumsily?

QUESTION

22. What is your attitude toward debt?

Be under obligation to no one—the only obligation you have is to love one another. (Romans 13:8a GNB)

The Western world is a consuming world. An individual, a family, even an institution is constantly urged to buy one thing or another. Advertising campaigns are sufficiently forceful that some persons are unable to resist acquisition pressures. Too often, the "buyers" are level-headed people who wish to be solvent and desire to avoid tension over money. But they are victimized. As some persons are "hooked" on alcohol or drugs, others are hooked on spending. They are "spendaholics." A few even buy things they do not want.

Some persons buy clothes they never wear or items they

cannot use. A number of buyers accumulate more than they can ever consume. And this sometimes leads to objectionable efforts to dispose of their purchases. Since they are constantly returning merchandise some stores have them spotted and reject their business. Others use different systems of disposing of items. Commonly, the items are stored for a time, given away to friends or one of the collecting agencies like the Salvation Army. Those agencies sometimes receive products in their original cartons, unopened. On occasion purchasers destroy or hide merchandise so that it will not be discovered by their mates.

Men and women who buy impulsively will battle debt for much of their early marriage experience. Their only escape will be to curb the buying impulse.

If couples could have drummed into them before marriage, "NO DEBT$ NO DEBT$ NO DEBT$" they would probably be much happier. Money arguments, which are the most common of all, would be greatly reduced. Mishandling funds creates disrespect among family members. Disrespect precedes disillusionment, and disillusionment, distrust. In that downward spiral a marriage may be doomed.

The "no debt" philosophy may, and usually should, yield on three items: education, home and transportation. Sometimes going into debt is a wise thing to do. If you go into debt to buy a house, you know you can always sell it to pay off your mortgage. And your car can usually be sold to pay off your car loan, if necessary. Likewise, if you invest in a college education, you are investing in yourself. Studies show the greater income and opportunities for advancement that follow an education make the investment a wise one. The car you buy does not need to be expensive, but it will be needed in many business or suburban situations. In each of the situations mentioned above the incurring of some debt is probably justified.

According to figures published in 1978, a young couple can expect to manage about $750,000 of personal money during their marriage. If the newlyweds could begin their planning imaginatively, with the money total of all their years in mind—a total larger than a small business would have managed in the 19th century—they might be willing to delay some immediate purchases to save for their future. That delay and review might cause them to save tens of thousands of dollars on debilitating habits and interest payments.

Assuming 50 years of marriage and two children, the average American couple will expend: Food—$113,000 (of which $26,000 will be eating out), Alcoholic Beverages—$5,000, Tobacco—$8,000, Housing—$159,000 (Home—$78,000, Operations—$28,000, Utilities and Fuel—$27,000, and Furniture/Equipment—$26,000), Clothing—$42,000, Transportation—$101,000 (Vehicles—$45,000, Financing—$5,000, Operating—$48,000, and Public Transportation—$3,000), Personal Care—$16,000, Health—$34,000, Recreation—$42,000, Books and Newspapers—$3,000, Education—$7,000, Insurance—$17,000, Gifts and Contributions—$27,000, Taxes, Savings, Investments—$163,000. The grand total of these expenses is $744,000.[33]

The Christian couple should review this list of averages in order to evaluate their long range spending priorities. Careful planning and early review in this area will help to avoid needless marital differences.

FOR DISCUSSION:
1. How much money do you have to launch this marriage?
2. What standard of living are you used to? What standard of living will you have after marriage?
3. In what circumstances would you agree to go into debt?

QUESTION

23. Have you considered a personal marriage contract?

In addition, Ruth the Moabite, Mahlon's widow, becomes my wife. This will keep the property in

the dead man's family, and his family line will
continue among his people and in his hometown.
You are witnesses to this today.
                                  (Ruth 4:10 GNB)

Marriage contracts are criticized by many idealists and counselors. Romantic traditions and bad publicity about some
contracts are at the root of the criticism. Marriage, they say, is
to be motivated by love and entered into with no reserva-
tions. They are doubly offended by those contracts which
permit sexual excursions with others, and have renewable
clauses within them. Man and wife renew, amend or reject
their contract every three to five years. Eminent and attractive authorities, like Amitai Etzioni of Columbia University,
object to marital contracts. It is to be hoped that, given the
situations Etzioni assumes, all persons would argue negatively about contracts.

However, contracts might be composed which would
leave out these objectionable elements. A contract, like life
insurance, may have no termination date, and the contract
may stipulate ideals rather than adaptations to human
weakness. For example, the contract prepared by Roger and
Janet Warmbir included eight articles: Authority, Division of
Labor, Children, Money, Sex, Religion, Personal Privacy,
and Miscellaneous. In it the couple stipulated Christian perceptions such as the husband "is the head of the house,"
there will be "four" children, a "budget book" is to be kept,
there will be "no extra-marital sexual activity," they will
"support the same church" and "take the children to
church."

Many other features were included in the agreement,
even to permitting alternate selections of paintings dis-
played in the home, protecting the privacy and social interests of both persons as individuals and as a couple. The
contract ended: "Each is expected to try to live in accordance
with Christian morality and to fulfill his obligations as a
citizen of the United States and to support the other in his
attempt.[34]

Although the Warmbir contract was composed in 1961, long before the liberation movement accented contracts which would modify traditional roles, it was designed to accentuate both the biblical roles and the basic rights of husband and wife in a relationship.

Historically, the marriage contract has been commonplace. Ancients contracted marriages between families. Fathers and uncles were well versed as negotiators. Boaz negotiated and contracted a levirate marriage for himself and Ruth which included the purchase of land. According to the customs of the times, he completed the business arrangement by using witnesses and removing his shoe to close the agreement. Some believe that, centuries later, the marriage of Joseph and Mary may have been contracted through the rules of the synagogue.

Matchmakers have been integral to some cultures. Dowries and family lands were sometimes incorporated in agreements. In early America there appeared a combination arrangement which connected choice (romantic exchange) of the young man and woman with parental guidance (permission). Many parents, by denying permission, prevented marriages.

There is a sense in which all marriages, even common law liaisons, are contracted. The official marriage license is a contract which can be broken by another contract, the divorce decree. Where no written contract exists, the exchange of oral promises between a man and a woman constitutes a verbal contract. Persons of integrity honor oral as well as written promises.

Upon our marriage my wife and I made several oral promises to each other which we have kept, and by which our marriage has advanced. For example, we promised each other that neither would resort to divorce court as a means for problem solving. That promise served well during a difficult period. Another agreement was that, although we would talk over any issues deemed important by either, she would have the last word on anything related to matters inside the house (furniture choices and arrangement), and I would have the final voice on anything outside (car or job). This division of responsibility did not emerge until a real crisis had developed, however.

Contracts are used in many high school and college courses on Marriage and the Family. The basic purpose of the contracts is to teach the art of negotiation, the art of getting along. Some therapists are using contracts to mend marriages that are on the verge of collapse. They are sometimes called "behavioral contracts" and focus on specific problems and sanctions. For example, "John will carry out the garbage every night or he will not play golf on Saturday." The agreement may be a trade-off, with the wife doing one thing as long as the husband does another. These agreements tend to fade out as new attitudes enter the marriage.

Other contracts may assist the children and help them carry responsibility. Duties of parents and children are observed by all the family members. The family becomes a loving corporation. Some personalities respond especially well to stipulations, even if those rules are loosely and casually formed.

The contracts which mean much to a society relate to high ideals, guarantees and privileges. The Constitution and the Bill of Rights are revered contracts. A birth certificate, driver's license, passport, even a ticket to a ball game, are contracts. There is a party of the first part and a party of the second part. Both of them give and both of them receive.

Society at large may be put off by a contract such as the one drawn up by Aristotle and Jackie Onassis, which is reputed to have had 170 articles in it. Another contract was drawn up by Elizabeth Bloomer and her groom before their marriage in 1948. Marian Christy reported the gist of this contract:

> We sat down before the wedding and, in a
> very businesslike way, defined our objectives.

> We decided, for example, on the number of
> children, and ardently agreed to the mutual
> promise that one would never try to "change"
> the other. We decided, too, a successful mar-
> riage is never really the 50-50 proposition it is
> chalked up to be. We settled for a 75-25 deal.
> Sometimes the 75 would emanate from my
> side. Sometimes it would have to be Jerry's
> gesture. We have carefully worked out the art
> of generous compromise.[35]

The point to be made here is that a contract may put one
or both members of the wedding at ease; later it might serve
to bridge a transition gap in a marriage or help in rearing
children. And it might be useful as a therapeutic method
during a difficult and threatening period.

Persons marrying again late in life, perhaps having lost
their first mates in death, may prepare contracts providing
for their heirs or distribution of their property. No personal
contract, even if it is drawn up by an attorney, will carry legal
force if it violates the letter or spirit of statutory law. For
example, if a bride agrees to disavow alimony in the event of
divorce, the agreement may not, and likely will not, stand
up in court.

Contracts, then, are as strong as the word and integrity of
the people who draw them up. They provide guidelines,
understanding, challenge and responsibility. It is taken as
appropriate that for centuries Christians, as a matter of
course, drew up personal covenants with God, and those
covenants served to deepen and develop those Christians.
Why then should there not be covenants drawn up between
bride and groom for the mutual benefit of their marriage?

FOR DISCUSSION:
1. Discuss some of the broad issues of marriage and ask
   yourselves, "Should we write out a marriage contract?"
2. What *specific* areas of married life do you think should be
   included in a contract?

24. How will you handle reverses?

His wife said to him, "You are still faithful as
ever, aren't you? Why don't you curse God and
die?"
*   Job answered, "You are talking nonsense!*
When God sends us something good, we
welcome it. How can we complain when he sends
us trouble?" Even in all this suffering Job said
nothing against God.   (Job 2:9-10 GNB)

During the course of a marriage couples will likely experience several reverses which threaten their marriage lives.
Loss of job, broken health, burglary, fire, death of a child are
serious reverses in a family. Reverses create havoc with
goals, expectations and the order of events. They may wipe
out all savings and force a couple into debt. They may cause
emotional stress leading to mental breakdown or further
tragedy. And suicide is not unknown in these circumstances.

How do couples confront reverses? Some totally collapse. They have no resources for emergencies. A husband
and wife lost their son in an air battle over Germany during
World War II. Before he was killed they were socially active,
church-related, hard-working. After they received word of
his death they withdrew, became embittered, and abandoned their church. They sold their home in Chicago and
moved to another community, rejecting their new neigh-
bors. They were unprepared to cope with a severe life-deal-
ing situation.

A common reve.   is the loss of health by one member of
the marriage. If it happens to the wife, and the husband is
unwilling to accept it, he may abandon her. If the marriage
was a long one, the woman may become bitter. If the marriage is young, the family of the invalid commonly enters the
case to assist and ease the suffering, loneliness and loss of

self-esteem. Until recent years, if circumstances were reversed between husband and wife, the wife nursed her husband. Presently it is not uncommon for women to abandon duty at about the same rate as men.

A common reversal occurs in job loss for the family breadwinner. During a couples conference the chairman requested the men to introduce themselves, their wives, tell what town they were from, refer to their children and occupation. One man, near the end of the series of statements, went through the list, concluding for "occupation": "I'm a zero. My job of 17 years ended in the recent recession, and I haven't been able to find anything." As he made the statement he glanced at his wife, and she cast a quick look at him. An observer could quickly tell that there was tension between them over the matter.

Later the story came out. The wife was unwilling to accept her husband's unemployment, had begun to nag him about getting another job, and appeared to have felt some derision for her husband in the delay. For the first time in his life the man was suffering severe loss of self-esteem. He needed loving support and encouragement, but his wife was not responding empathetically to the family problem. The man was not lazy, having proved himself until the loss of his job. His skills were well honed but limited. At his age he would find it difficult to find a position unrelated to his prior experience. There was a good chance that eventually he would find new employment and remain in the community he loved if the current distress could be weathered. But, because of his wife's lack of flexibility in this situation, a negative dimension crept into the marriage which could not be ignored. The marriage was not what it had been.

Some probing questions may be enlightening for many couples. The prospective groom might be asked, "What would you do if three years from now your family physician told you that your wife's health forbade further physical intimacy?" To this question many answers have been given, ranging from "I couldn't take that," to "I would discover resources in myself and in Christ to manage my life. I would remember that whatever I was going through was not as difficult as that which she was facing." There is a chasm of difference between the two answers. The first did not perceive the dimensions of his marriage vows. The second went beyond self and his own loss to the presumed ordeal of his wife.

Here are other questions which bear answering: "What would you do ... if he lost his job? ... if you lost your five-year-old child? ... if your new home burned down? ... if your silverware was stolen?" The answers to these questions tend to reveal the maturity levels in the couple, and they alert both persons to the hard facts of life which must be faced.

FOR DISCUSSION:
1. Are you ready to accept your share — fair or unfair — of dramatic problems?
2. How much life insurance should you have? Health insurance? Accident insurance?
3. Is your Christian faith solid enough to help you meet tragedy?

QUESTION
25. Where do you wish to live?

> *After Lot had left, the Lord said to Abram, "From where you are, look carefully in all directions. . . . Now, go and look over the whole land, because I am going to give it all to you."*
> *(Genesis 13:14, 17 GNB)*

Winston Churchill said, "We shape our buildings, and then they shape us." Some persons might share Churchill's perception more than others; they are deeply concerned about their surroundings. The type of house they live in—even the placing of furniture within the rooms—is vital to their sense of well-being and happiness. Their entire behavior as family members may be significantly influenced by their environment.

Before marriage a woman should express her feelings about the kind of residence she wants. Does she prefer city or suburban settings? If a city, a large or small one? Does she prefer an apartment or a house? How many rooms does she want? How are they to be furnished? Is the first home recognized as temporary? If so, how temporary is it? How does she feel about moving? What section of the country is her favorite? Where does she wish to settle and put down roots? Is she flexible to the demands of her husband's occupation?

Because a woman may spend more time in the home than her husband, she should have more to say about her needs within that home. One woman argued that she needed a house—"a place of my own, with grass around *all* of it." She felt she could not function in an apartment. Her husband, however, had no interest in doing the extra work required of a homeowner. It took a considerable amount of persuasion before he yielded to his wife's desires. They reached a happy compromise when the husband agreed to hire neighbor boys to do the yard work and other minor chores.

A counselor should point out the possibility—even the probability—that the couple's taste in houses may change as the years go on. A young bride may be willing to accept an apartment in a location she does not particularly like. At the outset she will accept other disadvantages. She may agree because her husband's occupation is not settled or he has to complete a college education. She may be working or a student herself, in which case she may want quarters which require little upkeep. The temporary nature of their situation causes husband and wife to feel gratified with modest living.

During this period one or more children may arrive. And this is not uncommon in student marriages. After a semester or two of trying circumstances the young wife phones for counseling. Tension has inflated beyond her control. Since the couple is too poor to engage a babysitter, she enters the office wrestling with her infant, and tries to describe her plight. Because of distractions concentration is difficult and, more often than not, the counseling session is unsatisfactory in almost every way.

In these cases the characteristics of collegiate marriages are often expressed in the words of one troubled young wife. The apartment is "too small," the wife is "hemmed in," and life becomes "dismal." Her husband's duties call for a study area, other human needs require still more space, and possessions accumulate as the family grows. The small apartment may be unkempt and prisonlike. The young couple— and their children, if any—may suffer claustrophobia, which damages family solidarity.

Certainly there are persons who fully enjoy apartment living and never wish to take on the larger responsibility of maintaining house and yard. Their only desire is to upgrade their situations from time to time, remaining in an accustomed life pattern. They enjoy urban living, use and enjoy cultural benefits provided by the community, and are free to travel more than their suburban friends. They are not as fearful of real or alleged crime threats as their suburban counterparts, nor do they choose the status symbols of those friends.

Some geographical preferences for living are made by persons because of childhood backgrounds, security considerations, cost of living, and the like. Counselors confront unhappy husbands and wives who never worked out personal preferences or requirements relative to city or rural sites, large or small houses, size of investment, buy or rent, old or new, renovate or not renovate.

American and Canadian families are mobile, moving more often than families in most other parts of the world. It is known that unless a family has lived 11 or more years in a home there is more than a 50-50 chance it will move.[36] Moves may take place as desires and needs for quarters change. Newly-marrieds "make do" for a time, shift into somewhat larger or upgraded places on ensuing moves, adding those features which they discover to be important to

their tastes and growing family. Attitudes change on preferences like kitchens and bathrooms. One bathroom will do at
the outset. Older couples, even those retired, often look for
homes or apartments with two baths. They tend to be less
flexible in their ways. When they move into a newer home or
apartment they tend to look for convenience more than a
"classy" neighborhood.

It is important that, before marriage, the prospective
bride and groom recognize those issues related to a lifetime
of changing personal and family interests. Mrs. Anne Morrow Lindbergh, wife of Charles Lindbergh, once stated that
a woman's life is broken up into 20-year periods. Enlarging
upon this idea on the 50th anniversary of her husband's solo
flight across the Atlantic, she said:

> We look upon men who seem to start here and
> go up on a kind of escalator to a plateau. They
> decide their careers and they just go up. Wom-
> en's lives aren't like that. They are educated,
> they have children, they have the slump, and
> they go up again. I think these periods of
> change are very creative. You only grow
> through change. [37]

Recognition of changing periods in the life of a wife who
bears children and adapts herself to the career of her husband may inspire that husband to become sensitive to the
needs and tastes of his wife relative to a choice for the family
residence. He should accommodate if he can. Occupational
requirements or other changing circumstances causing family displacement must be handled with care. Business
houses, church congregations and others who require geographical changes for their professionals have demonstrated
greater understanding and concern in recent years for family
relocations.

One study shows that death, divorce and moving are, in
that order, the three most traumatic experiences a family
encounters. And moving is a particular problem for children, a topic gaining attention in literature about family life.
More understanding is needed about the effects of residen-

tial changes upon wives and mothers as well as children. It is assumed that since men are less personally affected they are less concerned about moves. Someone once said that women are "nesters" and men are "perchers." Women are more likely to settle down, men to move on. In preparing for marriage the bride and groom should be aware of potential problems between them relative to the choice and nature of home and fireside.

FOR DISCUSSION:
1. Do you prefer urban, suburban or rural life?
2. Do you prefer house or apartment living?
3. Do you prefer owning or renting a home?
4. Do you have a time schedule for moving from one type of living situation to another?
5. Are you both aware of the financial burden which the different possibilities place upon you?

QUESTION

26. Do you know the difference between sex and love?

> *Now, to deal with the matters you wrote about.*
> *A man does well not to marry. But because there is so much immorality, every man should have his own wife, and every woman should have her own husband. A man should fulfill his duty as a husband, and a woman should fulfill her duty as a wife, and each should satisfy the other's needs. A wife is not the master of her own body, but her husband is; in the same way a husband is not the master of his own body, but the wife is.*   *(I Corinthians 7:1-4 GNB)*

Sex is an appetite. Love is not necessary for human participation in sexual activity. If love were required there could be no prostitution. Prostitutes actively resist love, for if they feel love for one of their customers they tend to withdraw from others. Sexual intercourse is not "making love" and, even in marriage, may not be an act of love. Sexual desire is, like hunger for food, a biological quest for gratification of an appetite. That appetite may be enhanced or reduced. Self-control, or lack of it, determines how large the appetite is permitted to grow.

Each human appetite for the Christian is controlled by a corresponding virtue. Appetite for food is appropriately controlled by moderation. With that control a person is advised to thank God for his provision and eat without fear. He may enjoy the experience of eating.

The appetite for sex should be controlled by the virtue of love. One of the most important characteristics of love is concern for the love object. When husband and wife relate their intimacy to their sincere concern for each other—which is sensitivity to the needs and tastes of the other—great problems will not likely occur in their sexual experiences.

Perhaps the culprit, relative to creating sexual tensions between mates, is the unrealistic expectation that varieties of physical intimacy will achieve perpetual ecstasy. Popular and pornographic literature distorts sex, but naïve and fantasy-making men and woman absorb the myth. They try to reproduce fantasy. They fail.

As a result, the enjoyment of sex is illusive in many marriages. In trying to develop compatibility, mates often add problems faster than solutions can be proposed. Feverish effort may lead to male impotency. It is sometimes caused by reducing sex to genital contact, overaccenting the importance of orgasm (mutual or individual), demanding responses created by fantasy, and believing that those responses rest upon physical gestures and actions rather than love and faith in oneself and spouse. Sex is made the be-all and end-all of man and woman relationships. The combination fails sooner or later.

The techniques and methodologies of sexual activity are widely circulated in excellent selected manuals. These may be reviewed easily and utilized as they are needed. They improve considerably the understanding of how husband and wife function in their intimacy.

One of the most significant meanings of sex is communication. When partners openly share—and continue to share—their feelings, concerns, questions, limitations, hopes and expectations, they will likely maintain a happy relationship. When verbal communication on the matter stops, intimacy is almost certain to decline.

Nonverbal gestures are best when they are lovingly aggressive and do what loving words say should be done. Genuine nonverbals ought not accent age or beauty, but love and value, which are offered in the human beings relating to one another. Wives ought to be as lovingly aggressive toward their husbands as they expect their husbands to be with them.

Following World War II, increased attention was devoted to research in marriage and family life. Old opinions were challenged by factual evidence. One of the first of these studies was completed by Dr. Paul Landis at Michigan State College (later Michigan State University). He studied 409 couples and discovered six points to be important to marriage: (1) sex relations, (2) spending family income, (3) recreation and social activities, (4) in-laws, (5) religious attitudes and (6) mutual friends. He stated that there had to be agreement on three of six to avoid shipwreck, four to be passably happy, all six to be thoroughly happy. The faster adjustments were made, the happier a couple would be. Both sexual and money issues took the longest to resolve. Not much change in these issues has occurred in the decades since the study.

FOR DISCUSSION:
1. What does sex mean to you?
2. Do you both believe in communicating your concerns and interests in sex?

3. Are you both aware that love is the virtue that ought to control your sexual intimacy?

4. Do you both believe that, no matter what emphasis you afford sexual intimacy now, it will change after marriage?

27. What will you do when you discover one partner is more highly sexed than the other?

One day Samson went down to Timnah, where he noticed a certain Philistine girl. He went back home and told his father and mother, "There is a Philistine girl down at Timnah who caught my attention. Get her for me; I want to marry her."
(Judges 14:1-2 GNB)
One day Samson went to the Philistine city of Gaza, where he met a prostitute and went to bed with her. . . . After this, Samson fell in love with a woman named Delilah, who lived in Sorek valley.
(Judges 16:1,4 GNB)

Although women's interests and participation in sexual activity is dramatically increasing (or is more openly acknowledged) all evidence shows that men remain more interested, more active and more demanding in sex than women. Only one in ten married women report greater sexual interest than their husbands.

The difference between men and women, little understood by either, is cause for considerable unhappiness. The greater expectations of the husband cause him to seek activity which, when rebuffed by his wife because of her lower interest levels, he interprets as unjustifiably rejected. He reacts. He may gradually withdraw from making gestures and advances. He may become angry even to the point of forcing his wife into relations with him. (The courts are in some instances treating this as rape.) Or, he may continue his marriage, taking whatever is dealt to him, and seek sexual experience with others. Or, he may deny his needs and enter a sexual limbo from which he may never emerge. Generally, the results of any of these responses are unfortunate, and may be tragic.

The specific patterns of sexual interest in women vary in the extreme, as they do for men, but a general pattern emerges. Women usually require more preparation for intimacy than men. They hope for a period during which assurance may be given that this experience relates to genuine affection and concern for the wife which incorporates sensitivity for womankind. At times this assurance is hard to give. Wives often remain unconvinced, sometimes for good reason and sometimes because they will not be persuaded. They are as lacking in perception about men as the husbands are about women.

After years of counseling men and women, I believe that shortly after the first weeks of marriage many wives begin to flag in their interest in sexual activity, principally in intercourse itself. The reasons for this shift are several, but a leading one seems to be that the marriage act is interpreted by some wives as degrading. They feel used, like a thing is used without sufficient regard for the thing itself. The marriage act appears to be highly desirable to their husbands, so desirable that whatever is the next best thing in marriage seems far down the attention ladder. If a wife feels that her value is as a thing to meet his "animal" needs, she may denigrate the experience. She feels like an object, and her interpretation reinforces her negative emotional feelings.

She is partly troubled about the matter because she both desires and does not desire intimacy at the same time. If the husband is crude in confronting her conflict, the likelihood of tension, accusation and recrimination in her is strong. He may become harsh and act in ways which further reinforce her negative suspicions about the whole business of marital sex.

A man's biological cycles, according to a report of a

significant number of men, occur in 48- to 72-hour repetitions. A man feels a need for intercourse in a two- to three-cycle week. His biological urges generally occur more often than those of his wife, although a wife, openmided on the matter, appears to adjust easily to his cycles. To do so, she must believe that the male has somewhat different motivations than her own, and those strong biological and psychological motivations are not evil or exploitive when expressed within the appropriate context of marriage.

In premarital counseling few prospective brides and grooms understand cycles in both sexual partners, although they are more aware of the menstrual cycle of the female, to which they must adapt. That there is a shorter, dynamic, insistent cycle in men is seldom understood or reviewed. When it is, women often adjust their thinking favorably, as do men. Prospective mates, when alerted, begin to deal with *needs*. And human beings are full of needs which, in many instances, can only be met by a mate who, under God, is "one flesh" with the other.

In marriage counseling situations one becomes aware of how little men and women know about sex. Perhaps a summary of specific statements will assist:

—About half of all married couples are confronted with deep sexual problems in their marriages.
—A surprising discovery (among many) is that one of the most common sexual problems is lack of desire. About seven out of ten wives do not experience orgasm through or during sexual intercourse. Insistence by couples on mutuality in physical response has led to considerable dissatisfaction.
—Of men who are impotent, perhaps ten percent or so are caused by physical or organic dysfunction. Nearly ninety percent of these problems are psychological in nature.
—There is no known age limitation for sexual participation between mates.
—Men, especially young men, who are sexually active re-

quire less time, sometimes very significantly less time, to become sexually aroused than women.

—No "normal" frequency for intercourse between husband and wife has been established, although there is a common pattern, referred to earlier, followed by a majority of couples.

—Fantasy or imaginative participation during physical relations between mates is common.

—No fixed length of time for each experience can be determined. Most complaints relate to shortness in sexual intimacy.

One additional point is important. Neither mate should disregard the personal tastes of the other. Both need to learn the art of intimacy with the other partner. No pattern of intimacy is the "right" one for a husband and wife—except the one they develop for themselves. It should not make any difference to them what intimate patterns anyone else evolves. If a wife is not comfortable with this or that gesture desired by the husband, the marriage ought to be able to survive that difference—and be happy. Mates are confronted with all kinds of exotic proposals by pornographers and sex researchers, which, if applied, are supposed to enhance, even save, their marriages. Many of those ideas emanate from persons with poor marriage records and they continue to cast about for even better ideas for the "bedroom Olympics."

It is known that, on the average, Christian marriages enjoy more satisfying intimacy than non-Christian. Perhaps this is because Christians are less interested in the intimate activities of others, and have greater concern for what is useful in their own marriage.

FOR DISCUSSION:
1. Are you aware of male cycles relative to sex?
2. Are you both aware of a woman's interests relative to sex?
3. How will these differences be treated?

28. What will you do if you discover your partner is romantically interested in another person?

*When the Lord saw that Leah was loved less
than Rachel, he made it possible for her to have
children, but Rachel remained childless. Leah
became pregnant and gave birth to a son. She
said, "The Lord has seen my trouble, and now
my husband will love me"; so she named him
Reuben.   (Genesis 29:31-32 GNB)
Stupidity is like a loud, ignorant, shameless
woman... "Come in, ignorant people!" To the
foolish man she says, "Stolen water is sweeter.
Stolen bread tastes better." Her victims do not
know that the people die who go to her house,
that those who have already entered are now
deep in the world of the dead.*
(Proverbs 9:13, 16-18 GNB)

A common human tendency which must be understood and
resisted is "erotic transfer." It seems that mankind is cursed
by erotic transfer. It may be present in any but the most
casual exchanges between men and women, and, in my
opinion, could account for most of the sexual feelings and
experiences that persons encounter. When two persons
meet, share mutual interests and respect each other, and
repeated conversational or social contacts result, the opportunity for erotic transfer has been provided. One needs
great integrity to be able to resist all temptations to violate
sexual fidelity in marriage.

Friends, parents, mates and children are close to us. We
know them well and need them. But that closeness, if
twisted, may become the cause of distresses which challenge
our moral purity. Incest, promiscuity or other sexual sin may
follow.

How do these situations develop? Who would be the most obvious choice for this "erotic transfer"? It could be anyone: the friend, or the doctor, or the minister, or the counselor, or the person at the next desk at a typewriter. This friend—professional or personal—seems gentle and understanding, perhaps warm and affectionate. The stage is easily set for distractions from meaningful treatment of real problems. Glances are exchanged, then gestures, then intimacy. Rationalizations begin to fly. Justification is made. Marriages are broken. Tragic consequences follow.

This destructive pattern need not develop. Falling into nearly certain temptation may be avoided by: (1) recognizing that the temptation of erotic transfer will happen, and not becoming distraught by the occurrence; (2) admitting as soon as possible to one's mate that outside attraction is present, and that help is needed from the mate to confront it; (3) insisting that physical attraction, no matter how innocently motivated, does not represent love and does not deserve to be so honored; and (4) keeping away from any contacts with the attractive third party with whom there appears to be an erotic transfer. Whatever may be the troubled person's problems they can and must be presented to another person who will remain objective and aloof of inherent danger.

No normal person is immune from the threat of erotic transfer. The desire to express sexual intimacy is strong, as is the desire to receive it. No matter what the protests may be to justify intimate transference, it is wrong and is the source of considerable mischief.

Catching transference early is helpful in solving the problem. Evidences that romance is cooling between husband and wife appear in many ways. Sleep habits provide an example. How an individual sleeps, according to researchers, reflects upon how he lives. A husband and wife soon establish patterns of sleep posture which reflect how they feel about each other. If romance between them is maintained, sleep gestures and positions will reinforce their identity with each other. (Certainly, there are legitimate reasons for some changes in patterns which are of no concern here.)

In his book, *Sleep Positions: The Night Language of the Body,* psychiatrist Samuel Dunkell reserves a volume of material for the effects of sleep upon marriage. Some of his case studies are tragi-comedy as men and women reflect the changes in their marriages through their sleep habits. Abrupt changes in those habits ought to signal vital information to a spouse.

If a marriage declines in sexual intimacy, husband and wife may physically but gradually move farther from each other. Some will become sufficiently adept at clinging to their own mattress edge that they will sleep in the same bed without touching even slightly. In one counseling session a man said, "You have no idea how big a king-sized bed is when you no longer have mutuality, much less intimacy. And it all started somewhere else, in an argument, or something."

Abrupt changes in sleeping habits may signal a romantic distraction in one of the mates. Persons with high levels of morality feel an obligation to be faithful to one person at a time. Even though married, a man or woman infatuated with another often feels the necessity of maintaining fidelity with the new romance, even though there may be no sexual dalliance. The unsuspecting mate is isolated and resisted. If the new romance continues, the innocent mate may be blamed. If necessary, fault in the innocent is manufactured by the distracted mate. And this will show up in changes in sleeping habits, eating patterns, conversational participation, schedule changes and in a score of other ways.

Wise mates, aware of human nature, will not permit situations to drift, but will, with tenderness and empathy, communicate concerns and insist on discovering what they may do to save and rectify relationships.

FOR DISCUSSION:
1. Is it likely that either or both marriage partners will sense a romantic interest for other persons?

2. Has this happened during your engagement period?
3. Does romantic appeal for another mean that true love has been transferred or is gone from a marriage?
4. What will you do if you feel the rise of romantic interest for another person during your marriage?

QUESTION

29. Do you plan on having children?

> If the Lord does not build the house, the work of
> the builders is useless; if the Lord does not protect
> the city, it does no good for the sentries to stand
> guard. It is useless to work so hard for a living,
> getting up early and going to bed late. For the
> Lord provides for those he loves, while they're
> asleep. Children are a gift from the Lord; they are
> a real blessing. The sons a man has when he is
> young are like arrows in a soldier's hand. Happy
> is the man who has many such arrows. He will
> never be defeated when he meets his enemies in
> the place of judgment.   (Psalm 127:1-5 GNB)

During the middle third of the 20th century, children and youth emerged to rule the social and family lives of some nations. More than most, the United States and Canada appeared to be caught up in the youth movement. Infants and little children were doted upon in many ways, but neglected in nurture. They were emancipated from the "seen-and-not-heard" generations before them. They were permitted to do as they pleased, floundered during their formative years, and were insufficiently nurtured in values, appreciation or self-discipline.

Children were not formed into adults. They were vaulted into adult experiences through contact with visual and sound media, debilitating habits and too much too soon. Little girls were given sexy Barbi dolls and facial makeup; they were urged to find boyfriends for dancing partners. Little boys were sometimes forced into playing Little League games like adults might play baseball, and they sampled beer and wine before their milk years were over. Alcoholism became a problem for many youths by the time they entered high school. Permissiveness became the standard for rearing youth.

With a vengeance, but without the resources of maturity, youngsters took to the grownup world. They entered a world of activity and made demands. Many became surly and rebellious. They made up the largest crime element in society. Denied their childhood and nurture, they rebelled against society partly by rejecting authority. This was observed in their attitudes in school, in rejection of the adult social world (choosing different grooming habits, work and language patterns and showing open distaste for their governments and other institutions).

These same young people, entering marriage, surprised counselors by stating that they desired to have no more than one or two children, and many said they wanted none at all. At first it was assumed that the decline in the commitment to children in marriage might be due to circumstances in the world—declining resources, atomic fallout threat, and other uncertainties. But couples did not affirm those reasons, except as marginal influences. The interests that emerged were the fear of rearing children like those in their own generation and the desire to be free of responsibility for children. Given the attitudes they observed in their peers, many young couples felt that it would not be personally rewarding to raise a family.

Nurturing children in the technological age appeared too difficult. Fear about rearing children was reflected in the disappointments young couples had experienced in relationships with their own parents. Premarriage couples were somewhat distressed about their own age group. Although supportive of their peers in public situations and in conflict with the common enemy, elders and authority figures, they privately were disillusioned with their own generation. They perceived it to be somewhat hedonistic, divided, polarized, undisciplined, unsure of itself and unhappy.

These young couples, anticipating marriage, are not sure about what kind of children they wish to raise. They have few models to emulate.

Young men and women, and older ones for that matter, do not realize that the golden age for nurturing children was back during a time when most families lived in a rural setting. Success was built into that environment. All family members were together for meals, work, church, simple recreation, birth, life and death. Educational needs were simple—readin', writin', 'n 'rithmetic. Religion played an important role. Government was small influence in life. Each person took care of the other. He had to; no one else would. The family was necessary, whereas modern life makes the family appear unnecessary. Family substitutes (government, remote work centers, schools, social services) do not provide happiness or a sense of belonging. Many betrothed couples feel, therefore, that remaining childless may offer them a more fulfilling life together.

The reason behind escaping the responsibility of rearing children is sometimes selfishness, sometimes economics, sometimes the result of women's liberation voices, sometimes fear, and sometimes the transitory quality of life introduced by couples living together without marriage. Many couples, married or cohabiting, want to be free from obligations to others so they can enjoy their independence, travel and do all the exciting things they haven't been able to do before.

Some prospective couples are aware of the costs of rearing children and shy from the duty for that reason. When children were workers on the farm they pulled their own weight. In the urban age they not only drain the family treasury but request large benefits which are luxury privileges in most societies. Even collegians who renounce materialism require more than their parents or grandparents did before them. They go to college in their own cars or with trailer loads of clothes, sports equipment, stereo sets and even furniture to substitute for dormitory furnishings.

Women's liberation literature created part of the anti-children feeling even among wives who were critical of some of the liberationist attitudes and goals. In bearing children women in large numbers were persuaded that they were put upon and unfairly treated. They complained they received too little assistance in caring for infants they did bear. For some, willingness to give birth was related to the promise of greater personal benefits, provisions of child care centers, and the like.

As cohabiting couples increased in number, birth rates declined. (And rates declined among marrieds, but not to the extent noted among common law marriages.) Unmarried couples experience low birth rates. Children of unwed couples face difficult problems, and many become wards of the state. But low birth rates among unmarrieds mean only that a potentially catastrophic problem has been somewhat minimized.

Men and women on the threshold of matrimony should take time to sift out their contradictions about children. How many will they bear? When will they bear them? Are they willing to devote the energy and time that success with children requires? Are they willing to run against the tide of their own personal interest? Are they willing to do what they ought to do to assure wholesome neighborhoods, effective schools and sound churches? Are they willing to nurture in a manner which accents what is best for their children? Do they feel that their children should measure up or perform (school grades, athletics, popularity) to gratify the parents or meet the needs of the children?

It should be noted that birth rates rise and fall with changing attitudes and social circumstances. During the Great Depression of the 1930s the rate fell. World War II stimulated a baby boom. With the disillusionment in the mid-1960s, the rate plummeted. Influences may be expected to arise that will turn the pattern in another direction. Increase and decrease will follow each other. History is told in cycles.

In the end, most couples acknowledge that children are

worth the effort. We need them; they need us. It is interesting to note that a parental urge is common, so common that it may be expected to emerge for the vast majority of couples. During premarital counseling, a man and woman may rule out the possibility of having children. Later on, however, the desire for them may be expected to rise and biology will take its course. If the desire becomes strong for one and weak for the other, tension will likely ensue. Even so, children in goodly numbers will be born and reared at any cost and through any danger.

For all time, the questions listed here remain vital and relevant to Christian brides and grooms. What they say and do about children often reveals their faith and life goals.

FOR DISCUSSION:
1. How many children do you plan to have?
2. When are they planned for?
3. If no children are planned, is the motivation Christian?
4. Are you both willing to reopen discussion about children after a few years of marriage?

QUESTION

30. What is your feeling about birth control?

Michal, Saul's daughter, never had any
children.   *(2 Samuel 6:23 GNB)*

Christians contemplating marriage often ask, "Where in the Bible is there any guidance about birth control?" There are no specifics relative to the matter in the Scriptures. However, marrieds are not left without some instruction.

Certainly God controlled births in a number of special instances reported in the Bible. Wives were kept from pregnancy by the Lord, and later were permitted pregnancy. Isaac, Samson and Samuel were born to women who were past the age of bearing and had never had any previous

children. Other women, like Leah, were permitted many
children, whereas God limited the pregnancies of Rachel,
her sister. The love acknowledged between Jacob and Rachel
is reason enough to believe they had more intimate experiences than did Jacob with Leah. (Leah negotiated with
Rachel for more time with Jacob.) The point made is that God
permitted or denied pregnancy. Pregnancy historically has
been regarded as an act of God.

Opponents of birth control argue that this is precisely the
point—God decides, not human beings. But arguments
about God's providences in human behavior are troublesome when cast as absolutes. If rain does not fall, is a farmer
justified in irrigating his crops? If too much rain falls, is man
justified in damming up the excess? If a person is ill, is he
justified in using medication? If he is ill, is he justified in
refusing medication?

There is an obvious sense in which pregnancy is a
biological matter. Perhaps, in the providence of God, it may
be helped or hindered through medical technology. Rachel,
in competition with her sister, insisted upon another child.
In giving birth to Benjamin, she died. In our time a physician
might well have discouraged Rachel from bearing children—
at least her last one. Or, by medical intervention, saved her
life. All this suggests that in the collision of human biology
and technology with divine providence man is not fully
informed. He must do the best he can as a moral being in
concluding some matters.

Birth control is an ancient practice. Some of the methods
adopted in premodern days appear crude and unsophisti-
cated by current standards. It is highly probable that the
ancients would believe some current practices crude and
inhumane. For example, nothing in the Scriptures justifies
abortion as a means for birth control. No method used by
men and women controlling their own destinies in historical
times appears as unsatisfactory as abortion. (We don't know
how widely abortion was practiced in the ancient world.)

All rights incur risks and privileges. Participation in life
carries duty. And those who take the privilege of sexual

intimacy or any other human privilege should be willing to accept the consequences of their acts. This may include pregnancy, birth and rearing children. There is no biblical implication that, once generated, embryonic life can be terminated with moral approval. Yet there may well be medical reasons for terminating a pregnancy. Special cases, however, shouldn't determine normative ethics.

Some forms of birth control appear to be objectionable because they violate the concept of control. They are used to prohibit pregnancy altogether. It is hard to accept interuterine devices or vasectomies if the purpose is to totally avoid pregnancy during an entire marriage. The interuterine device is foreign to the anatomy of women. Its continuous presence invites adhesions and other problems, including psychological ones. A number of physicians, for reasons of conscience, have expressed objections to the device with nearly the vehemence some have reserved for abortion.

Vasectomy may be appropriate to a husband who, having fathered children, might for the sake of his wife agree to the operation. Reproductive sex, having achieved its purpose, is surrendered without giving up unitive sex.

There are two matters in all these considerations: (1) birth control is planning, not prevention; and (2) each mate is considerate of the concerns and needs of the other.

It is presumed that most couples practice birth control in order to space their children. Some forms of control reduce the ability to become pregnant when the control method is withdrawn. This factor must be considered in family planning. This is generally a temporary phenomenon, but may require medical attention.

If a couple, for the sake of health or special circumstances feel they should not generate children, and they review their motivations satisfactorily with a spiritual counselor, they might design their lives and intimacy according to the special needs. They owe some of their lives to the next generation, and they must be free of selfishness. Couples should show cause for avoiding the generation of children.

There are effective means for birth control. Couples need

to be well advised. And when such decisions are made a competent physician should monitor the effect on both husband and wife. Because this or that method appears to have statistical advantage and general convenience is no assurance that its prescription will serve every couple equally well.

Too little consideration is given to natural means for controlling pregnancy. For many decades the rhythm method was advocated by the Roman Catholic church, but many couples did not stick to it. They found it difficult to avoid sexual intimacy during a wife's fertile period. Many women reported success for the "rhythm method" but were not believed. Recently new voices have defended the old and natural means for birth control, based on appropriate self-control. The benefits appear to go beyond the management of pregnancy, and relate to a couple's sense of well-being.[38]

FOR DISCUSSION:
1. Are you well advised about birth control methods for your case?
2. Are you going to be monitored by a physician?
3. Are you agreed on all issues of birth control?
4. Do you know the difference between birth control and birth prevention?

QUESTION

31. Are you flexible?

In the same way you wives must submit yourselves to your husbands, so that if any of them do not believe God's word, your conduct will win them over to believe. It will not be necessary for you to say a word, because they will see how pure and reverent your conduct is. You should not use outward aids to make yourself beautiful, such as the way you fix your hair, or the jewelry you put on, or the dresses you wear.

*Instead, your beauty should consist of your true
inner self, the ageless beauty of a gentle and quiet
spirit, which is of the greatest value in God's sight.*
                                    (1 Peter 3:1-4 GNB)

Flexibility is indispensible to a good marriage. Flexible persons are not only happy themselves, they are able to create an atmosphere conducive to the happiness of others. Inflexible persons are, understandably, the opposite. They are rigid, see matters in black and white, and are often judgmental of others. They do not see the differences in personalities and circumstances. For one to accept those differences shows respect for variety in human experience.

Suppose that an evening out has been on the schedule for some time. The wife has planned for the occasion and looked forward to it. By midafternoon she has nearly completed personal grooming and the preparation of her clothes. Just then her husband calls and regretfully informs her that company demands prevent him from carrying through on their plans.

If the wife is inflexible, she will express her disappointment in tones that communicate deep wounds; she may recite the extent of preparations which are for nought; and she may be accusatory of her husband or his company. She may bring up promises made and not kept, family priorities, the love focus. The broken event is criminalized. Perhaps tension and arguments follow. For several days recriminations may characterize the marriage.

The flexible wife accepts emergency, encourages her mate who is caught between two responsibilities, and designs a satisfactory alternative for her evening. She remembers that her husband does not break promises without good reason. (If indeed he is not habitual in breaking promises.) Disappointments do not occur often. Another date will be set soon to carry through a delayed celebration. Because of these generous attitudes, both parties can make the substitute date a better one than the first might have been. (The story and application of flexibility could be told in the same way for husbands and children.)

Flexible persons generally understand human weaknesses and are willing to accept and adjust to them. Flexible mates refuse to jeopardize their marriage because he does not hang up his clothes as regularly as he should, or she fails to have dinner prepared on time every evening. Whatever the occasion they can shift to early or late, to slower or faster, to less or more. They do not feel undue imposition in giving up something preferred. They are willing to please, and do not feel specially virtuous in doing so. Inconvenience is as much a part of life as any other aspect.

FOR DISCUSSION:
1. Are you flexible?
2. Which of you is the more flexible?
3. Are there boundaries or limitations to flexibility?

QUESTION
32. Do you share the same interests?

> *The boys grew up, and Esau became a skilled hunter, a man who loved the outdoors, but Jacob was a quiet man who stayed at home. Isaac preferred Esau because he enjoyed eating the animals Esau killed, but Rebecca preferred Jacob.*
> *(Genesis 25:27-28 GNB)*

The question really is, do you have mutuality? Or, do you have togetherness? Or, when there is opportunity to choose an activity, are your interests similar or different? How do both of you feel about sports, hiking, television, music, reading, sleeping, household chores, hobbies, church, education, conversation, friends and rituals?

One might begin with a discussion of rituals. What would you like to do every Thanksgiving Day, every Christmas? The turkey, oyster dressing, cutting the Christmas tree, exchanging gifts, hunting eggs, traveling on a camping trip, prayers before bedtime, and a thousand other rituals may become a part of the family. In our home we nearly always eat out after church on Sundays. We always fill huge stockings at Christmastime. These are rituals. Strangers looking into our home on any such occasion know something special is taking place.

One of the reasons for family collapse is the decline of ritual in the family. Families often lose solidarity because they lose mutuality. They no longer go to church together, eat together, vacation together, and the like. Without ritual, family ties inevitably weaken. Children are enchanted by rituals. They fantasize about them, staying awake joyfully, speculating on the outcomes. Vivid memories are built on the fairylike atmosphere that happy rituals create. Currently there are millions of children without family rituals. So they create new ones in peer gangs.

The first easy rituals for children of Christian parents relate to church and prayers. Very close to those appear holidays and birthdays, which raise strong competition to the first religious rituals. Combinations of rituals can be designed. My wife or I prayed with our children at bedtimes, and they played church on Sunday mornings. On Thanksgiving Day, following the feast, each person around the table expressed thankfulness for one thing that happened during the year, or something deeply felt. And because no experiences could be repeated in the round, when it came to my turn at last, I would have to think of something really different from the expected. My thankfulness was not merely for the children or my wife, but for some exotic truth which identified and gratified our family. One night a week the family watched a television show and ate tossed salad. During warm summers a picnic a month was planned—always with potato salad and cold chicken.

Readers of biography may pick up the rituals which tied eminent persons to their families. When I was a lad, President Franklin D. Roosevelt read Dickens' "The Christmas Carol" to his family on Christmas Eve. The reading was sometimes aired over the radio. I later memorized it and repeated it for many Christmases as an interpretive reading.

During the 1930s Mayor Fiorello La Guardia of New York City read the "funnies" over the radio to children and families on Sunday. I recall his vivid descriptions. He was particularly fond of "Li'l Orphan Annie." Perhaps his reading had something to do with stimulating the popular song named after the comic strip.

When a man and woman marry they bring together ritual and tradition from two families. Some rituals collide, so choices must be made and should be made in good grace. Must every Christmas be spent at her parents' house? Perhaps alternate holidays may be selected. Considerate persons may find it hard to believe that marriages may experience deep unhappiness and weeks of retribution when some treasured family ritual is violated or modified. Of course it is not possible to continue all the rituals of each family from one generation to another. For it would not be long before there would be too many to adopt. What is a great blessing can become, with a little human effort, a curse.

Many interests draw husband and wife together, and these constitute the elements of mutuality. Both may engage in the same profession, enjoy their children and share in the same religious faith. Or they may find mutuality by doing different things at the same time. For example, while he watches television she practices the piano in another part of the house. Or they may complement each other in that he may enjoy earning money and she may enjoy spending; he expects an attractively groomed wife and she make a hobby of being a "clothes horse."

Lack of mutuality may become serious in a marriage in which one mate is committed to something in which the partner is not only disinterested but even disdainful. If a man who is interested in art and has studied it seriously is married to a woman who makes disparaging remarks about art, a serious breach in mutuality will occur. And that rift, if emphasized by either mate, often takes away or threatens other areas where mutuality might otherwise have been cultivated. In some instances the lack of mutual interest in one major area can destroy a marriage.

Some individual interests create serious dissonance, such as one mate enjoying social experiences often and with many friends, whereas the partner finds privacy and escape from people necessary for a sense of personal well-being. Tension between mates is often great under such divergent circumstances. Maturity and flexibility can save marriages of this type, but many persons lack those qualities.

Still other mutuality failures grow out of attempts by either party to please the other by faking interest during courtship. After marriage the genuine person emerges, returning to first habits. Tension follows. Both mates may feel cheated. This kind of pretence dries up otherwise promising circumstances. Such a case involved a man who liked horses. He raised them, rode them, prepared them for show. His wife enjoyed the interest, or affirmed that she did, at first, but gradually withdrew. Ultimately, he abandoned her and married a woman who would share his interest.

Mrs. Charles A. Lindbergh, following the death of her husband in 1974, broke away from the intense privacy which had been so meaningful to her husband and habitual for the Lindbergh family. In a television interview with commentator Eric Sevareid, she revealed how she forced herself to adapt to her husband's interest in flying about the world during the early days of aviation. She rode in the back cockpit, often paralyzed with fear, but determined to be a part of her husband's experience. (He had parachuted four times from disabled planes before his Atlantic flight. He was on the verge of being grounded by aviation authorities when he made his fabled flight.)

A remarkable woman, Anne Morrow Lingbergh was an important influence and sometime leveler of her husband's

passion for air adventure and for his crusades, some of
which failed. Her selfless devotion to the pursuit of mutuality serves as an example to men and women alike. It is
through a similar determined effort that one contributes to a
happy marriage. Her husband also adapted to her interests
by assisting her in her literary efforts. She created magnifi-
cent pieces, like *Gift from the Sea*. It is also likely that she
inspired and helped him in the course of the writing that he
accomplished.

FOR DISCUSSION:
1. In what ways do you share high mutuality quotients?
2. In what ways are they low?
3. Do you have a plan to develop mutuality?
4. If mutuality fails, how will you deal with it?

QUESTION

33. What is your attitude toward household chores?

> *She keeps herself busy making wool and linen
> cloth.*
> *She gets up before daylight to prepare food
> for her family and to tell her servant girls what
> to do.*
> *She spins her own thread and weaves her
> own cloth.*
> *She's always busy and looks after her family's
> needs.*   *(Proverbs 31:13, 15, 19, 27 GNB)*

If the popular communication media are to be believed,
domesticity has fallen upon hard times. Home and fireside
are sometimes derided. Liberationists complain that women
are victims of inequality because of domesticity. Some complaints are justified, but some distort family life and
privilege. A housewife is "merely" a housewife, and her
status is presumed to be that of a slave, lackey, and mindless

mother. She is victimized by men in general, and her husband in particular. Her tasks are nearly meaningless, repetitive and boring. She needs to be liberated. So follow the strident claims of new crusaders.

It is not clear why some movements feel they must put down legitimate roles in order to achieve status for their own, but they do. Because of the criticism of traditional family patterns, a housewife may feel guilty about her dedication to the care of home, husband and children.

One way of creating unhappiness for a housewife is to so derogate household chores that a woman is made to feel moronic if she devotes much time to them or fails to shuck many of them off to other family members. Housekeeping is equated with drudgery. Most polls show that domestic chores are believed to be the least attractive of all jobs. There is reason to believe that critics of domesticity are responsible for the low opinion. The detractors do not point out that most jobs outside the home are less varied, even less satisfying, than home chores. The work of a housewife is as varied as most employment outside the home.

One of the most common complaints of husbands to counselors relates to the general condition of home quarters. Unmade beds, unkempt homes, unwashed dishes, and the like reflect negatively on unorganized persons. Happy attitudes from husband and children are sometimes traceable to the quality of life in a home. The effective keeper of the house deserves credit for an important function. Knowledge of the importance of excellent homemaking should be gained before marriage.

The division of family labor is sometimes related to stereotyped male and female images. Housework is not reserved for women; neither is yard work nor repair problems for men. Traditional assignments may be traded off. Most prospective mates, however, state in premarital counseling that they prefer the traditional division of labor if each is considerate of the other's problems. Investigation shows that husbands are less likely to fulfill their domestic assignments than women. The plea for a reasonable sharing of household responsibilities when the wife also holds down a full-time job is one that ought to be heard.

As a housewife is not limited to her home, so a husband is not confined to his occupation. There is a lawn to be cut, a house to be painted, windows to be washed, screens to be installed, repairs to be made, and other chores to be shared. In short, there is a domestic role for each family member. Those roles should include menial as well as major tasks for children as well as parents.

Perhaps the most significant issue relative to household chores is for parents to respect their importance and teach their children to assist in doing them. A daughter should be taught to cook as well as clean her room. A son should help paint the house as well as carry out the garbage. From time to time the boys should shift assignments with their sisters. Children feel happier about their jobs when they realize they are helping to keep their house and yard attractive. The business of the home must be organized. Done in an orderly manner, domestic duties are completed and family solidarity is strengthened in the process.

FOR DISCUSSION:
1. Do both wife and husband consider housekeeping and household chores worthy of their time?
2. Is it appropriate to assign priority responsibility for each chore to one member of the family?
3. Are male and female images restricted to certain household assignments?

QUESTION

34. What do you expect of each other?

Sarah was like that; she obeyed Abraham and called him her master. You are now her daughters if you do good and are not afraid of anything.

In the same way you husbands must live
with your wives with the proper understanding
that they are the weaker sex. Treat them with
respect, because they will also receive, together
with you, God's gift of life. Do this so that
nothing will interfere with your prayers.
(I Peter 3:6-7 GNB)

Unrealistic expectations may be the termites of marriage. They possess the ability to undermine it little by little. We see this erosion in the young bride who presumes that she will not be confronted by large problems in sex relationships, money management or child-rearing. She finds it difficult to anticipate boredom, uncertainty and a different life pattern in marriage.

Although her groom has received little education for marriage, a wife expects that he will be consistent and gracious with her. He will be patient, slow to anger, willing to comfort her in moments of depression, supportive in her decisions, reinforcing her self-esteem. She is surprised and hurt that he is not that sensitive. He is unaware that so much is expected of him.

No one goes into marriage prepared for its repetitions, its labor, its human limitations. No amount of warning, counseling, or observing other marriages raises the awareness sufficiently to save the bride from disappointment. In bewildered tones, she declares, "Marriage isn't what I expected it to be."

Part of her difficulty—as well as his—relates to the human ability to hope, to understand, to expect more from life and friends or family members than they can produce. The closer the relationship, the higher the expectation. When aspirations fail, disappointment follows. Ideals appear to have been violated. Disillusionment sets in.

Each marriage possesses its own uniqueness. Combinations of characteristics created by the marriage of two people, themselves unique, are not likely to be recognized at the outset of married life. Soon each member of the wedding begins to make discoveries about the other's interests and

habits. These tend to offend because they require unexpected and sometimes unusual effort and patience from
each.

In themselves, the differences in biology between a man
and a woman are great enough to create tension. Add differences in rearing, education, hobbies, perceptions and scores
of other factors, and the stage is set for comedy and tragedy.

We see this tension in the following hypothetical case. A
young woman has been conditioned by a Victorian, gentle,
conservative, and protected environment of a fairly affluent
home. She meets a young man whose environment has
been casual, worldly, and competitive. Even though she
capitulates to his appeal, her tolerance for deviation from the
"norm" are limited in contrast to his. She is more likely to be
jealous, to feel injured at slights, and to be sensitive about
moral issues.

During the engagement period the woman finds the
differences tolerable, even attractive. They provide variety to
her former experience. They make the relationship dramatic,
and flavor is added to romantic activity. The young man, in a
"mating dance" spirit, is not really himself. He is solicitous,
forgiving of her conservatism, adaptable in specific instances. After marriage his real self emerges. He does not
maintain his special courting self.

The new bride expects her husband to ask no more of her
than she is willing to give—in sex, in housework, in mutuality, in anything. He is supposed to be wise to sense what the
comfortable limits are for her. He likely will fail. And what
may be failure to the point of becoming intolerable for one is
a foible of humanity to be laughed about for another. If
differences in acceptance levels are too great, the chances for
happiness are reduced or lost.

The prospective bride should be very explicit about matters which are vital to her, matters which she can identify,
and suggest responses which make her comfortable. One
woman clung to several small superstitions which she
apologized for, but made clear were important. The husband-to-be laughed at some of them but catered to all. After

marriage those same laughable beliefs irritated him. He made it clear that he expected his wife to "grow up" and the foibles to pass. The stage was set for further trouble because each one felt that he was right in his feelings.

In another case the bride expected that all domestic chores related to preparation of meals or internal housekeeping were her responsibility. Her husband enjoyed helping, especially vacuuming the floors. But his wife felt that his participation was a means of criticizing the quality of her work. She not only wished to have labor roles clearly divided, including the shopping chores, but she expected her husband to leave the room in which she was working. He wished for intimacy in working together with his wife; she wished for exclusiveness in order to build up confidence in herself as a competent homemaker. Both persons interpreted each other incorrectly.

Often the tragic part of these differences is the assumption that failure to meet expectations means that love has failed, and that one's partner is not what he was perceived to be. These feelings result in an almost irresistible desire to end the marriage. Through premarital counseling the threat may be blunted.

Mary Richard, a counselor, has developed a program which she uses with persons anticipating marriage. She suggests that they "be as quick to praise as criticize; evaluate without devaluating." She reminds them, "Always remember each of us is unique so our response (and reaction) to life will be unique too." Because of this, everyone should "clear the machine many times daily, which is forgiveness-on-the-spot." This means that each minor irritation should be dealt with immediately before it develops into a major issue. This is not easy to do. But no one has promised that marrige would be easy. What is promised is that the results are worth the effort.

All, or nearly all, of the implications of this particular question applies to both marriage partners. Both persons are involved. The following list points out some possible differences:

	EXPECTATIONS		INTERPRETATIONS	
	His	Hers	His	Hers
SEX	Intense	Moderate	She doesn't love me.	He uses me.
MONEY	Spender	Saver	She doesn't want to have any fun.	He is immature.
HOME	Castle	House	She is sloppy.	He puts too much value on it.
CHILDREN	Assumed	Anticipated	She cares more for the baby than she does for me.	He is selfish and should be happy with half my time.
DISCIPLINE	Stern	Permissive	She will spoil the children rotten.	He is unjust and too severe.
IN-LAWS	Casual	Attached	She is tied to her mother's apron strings.	He is insensitive and unappreciative.
GROOMING	Sloppy	Careful	She thinks clothes are too important.	He is a slob.

HABITS	Careless	Controlled	She is excessively strict about life.	He is weak.
ATTITUDES	Easygoing	Intense	She is uptight.	He is irresponsible.
PEOPLE	Friendly	Private	She is nonsocial.	He avoids his family and other relationships.
WORK (His)	Interested	Disinterested	She is not interested in the things I do.	He puts his work ahead of me.
WORK (Hers)	Disinterested	Interested	She doesn't do much during the day.	He doesn't put value on what I do.
RECREATION	Athletic	Unathletic	She won't try anything.	He is never going to grow up.
RELIGION	Insincere	Sincere	She is a goody-goody.	He is a hypocrite
COMMUNICATION	Spasmodic	Vital	She babbles all the time.	He doesn't love me or he would talk to me.
LANGUAGE	Precise	Ungrammatical	She is ignorant.	He is picky-picky.

As human beings we tend to downgrade our fellow human beings. When we criticize another person, we may choose to be positive or negative, but in most cases we choose to be negative. When this tendency influences a marriage, it may threaten its very existence.

The early generations of this nation faced unimaginable hardships, deprivations, setbacks. People who married in those days must have experienced tensions, incompatibility and other problems. Yet they felt committed to their mates. It was only as the nation began to develop that the expectations of married couples began to rise excessively. But expectations implied responsibilities which were at first carried.

Since World War II and the easy provision for education, the glut of manufactured goods and a philosophy of plenty, many persons—especially among the most recent generation of things we want. We can buy whatever we wish. If we tlement means that we have a high standard of living and privileges which we see as rights without accepting the responsibilities they imply. Unlike our ancestors, we don't need to work and save for purchases, or delay the acquisition of things we want. We can buy whatever we want. If we don't get what we want, someone else is to blame. But a marriage cannot succeed when such an attitude exists. Newlyweds who assume they have the right to happiness will soon be disappointed. Unless they change, their marriages have little chance of success.

FOR DISCUSSION:
1. As a wife, do you have any expectations of your husband that he may not understand? What are these expectations?
2. As a husband, do you have any expectations of your wife that she may not understand? What are these expectations?
3. What expectations and interpretations representing your relationship could be added to the above list?
4. What affirmative interpretations may replace the negative ones listed above?

35. Do you wish to grow old with this changing person?

Sarah lived to be 127 years old. She died in
Hebron in the land of Canaan, and Abraham
mourned her death.

(Genesis 23:1-2 GNB)

Persons change, and significantly so. Men who were aggressive, hard-working, even domineering over their families, may at retirement become gentle, even reserved. Some withdraw from business and enjoy a casual life they believe they earned. They fantasized about their retirement years for one or two decades and may have chosen to quit professional life earlier than the average person. It is not uncommon for military or other government personnel to retire after 20 or 30 years of service. Many men stop working in their early or mid-50s.

The wife of such a man is sometimes shocked by the course of events. She is irritated to have him "under foot" all the time. She discovers he is willing, and may be eager, to give up his former role. He may drop physical intimacy with his wife. He may leave money management and decision-making to her. He treats the grandchildren differently (better) than he treated his own offspring. He may become slovenly and expect to be waited on more than ever before.

Many men do not relish their roles during their productive years, but they determine to do their duty. When the time comes, they are pleased to chuck the whole obligation. Others achieve their goals, prove they can "make it," and withdraw from the field as they see ambitious young men jockeying for their jobs. When children are reared and responsibilities as provider have been carried out, a husband may no longer be motivated by family duties.

At the same point in time many women no longer feel they should be homebound, sensitive and gentle, or obliging to every family member. They may become poor house-keepers or, without children to clutter, become immaculate for their own gratification and appearances of achievement.

The point to be made is that persons may change dramatically. That is one of the risks of marriage. Some of those changes are attractive and others unattractive. Yet acceptance of each other by husband and wife should be sufficiently deep to include all that will happen to each mate in future time.

Futurism should be discussed by prospective mates. Futurism here refers not to life after death, but that natural life which persons share together through several decades until death.

One of the most troublesome changes which arise during the later years of a marriage relates to health decline. Decline may be physical and/or mental. If one mate encounters illness, the intimacy and closeness which were standard for the couple during early years may be weakened or ended. Each mate may become independent of the other. For some marriages the strain is too great. Old people get divorces, too.

Some persons become frail in body, retaining alert minds; others remain robust, with failing mental powers. A long and happy marriage may be turned into a ghost relationship as a mate loses orientation. That person, formerly loving and dutiful, may accuse the competent mate of plotting to murder him, steal family assets or abandon him. Suspicion and awareness of one's own frailty may cause unfortunate changes in a person.

The death of a family member, personal disfigurement, emotional stress, alleged awareness and a score of other influences may change a mate to the point that the person emerging from these circumstances is nearly unrecognizable. A woman totally committed to her husband and children for years was persuaded in middle life that her status was menial and she should become a liberated woman. She was willing to stay married but insisted on a revision of all family organization. The husband was faced with a different, if not new, marriage. He adjusted to save his home. The children remaining in the home never adapted to the changes. What had been a happy family became unhappy and tense.

In another marriage the husband, formerly a Christian worker in a youth movement, decided that he should be freed from total continuity with his wife and child. He did not seek divorce but did choose to live a portion of the week at home and a portion in his private apartment. He dropped his religious activities but became committed to secular service. His wife was faced with a new kind of marriage if she was to keep it at all. She adapted well, but there always seemed to be something missing which was needed if memories were to be happy ones.

Society does not yet seem to know much about aging. Persons seem afraid of it. Students of history believe that, according to Dr. Bob Young, "one-third of all the people that have ever reached the age of 65 are alive right now." The modern move by some persons against legal marriage is partly motivated by an unwillingness of the advocates to be tied down to changing circumstances, to care for a drooling invalid mate, to deny one's own wishes and expectations because of the withdrawal of a mate in physical decline. For these persons, marriage would be acceptable in health, but not in sickness; in wealth, but not in poverty; for better, but not for worse. Common-law or casual cohabitation relationships generally are concluded when one or the other member in the agreement is in serious personal difficulty.

Marriage, if it is Christian, includes the acceptance of the possibility that one's mate changes and those changes may occur without destroying the marriage. That one may become an invalid and the other may be called upon to serve sacrificially is a possibility. Who knows who is going to be served, who is going to serve? And if the choice is left to an informed Christian mate, who would not choose to serve? Marriage should carry with it elements of an insurance policy, a shared risk. One takes on the risk of investment, and may expect the benefit of gain if circumstances don't go against him. His "loss" in the risk is his responsibility carried in the event of the failure of his wife's health. His gain is the care his wife affords him if he should lose his.

Even with problems of aging, the probabilities are high for happiness in a marriage that survives a couple's middle years. At this writing only five percent of American elders are in nursing homes or other institutions. Perhaps twice that number ought to be given institutional help. That leaves as much as 90 percent of our senior citizens in private dwellings. Only five percent pull up stakes on retirement and move to warm climates. More than half the elders live with their spouses in their own homes in the communities in which they lived during their late middle years.

I know a man 100 years old who is living with his 89 year old wife in the home they chose for retirement. The couple live alone near their son, and each member cares for the other, vigorously resists being moved, and appears supremely happy. The pair provides inspiration to all who know them—they never give up living to the fullest, and it appears that they never will as long as strength and wits remain.

FOR DISCUSSION:
1. How much change do you believe your marriage will encounter?
2. How much risk are you both willing to take for the unknown marriage ahead?
3. How do you feel about growing old? About growing old together?

QUESTION

36. How do you handle your partner's success or failure?

God created them male and female, blessed them, and named them, "Mankind."

(Genesis 5:2 GNB)

"The twain shall be one flesh" is an oft-repeated marriage phrase, the meaning of which is sometimes elusive. There are special and varied meanings for the phrase. One of these is mutual identity of husband and wife. That identity is, or ought to be, dynamic to the point that a person is not separately defined from his or her mate. The idea is readily perceived by anyone acquainted with happily married persons. One's memory of the woman is immediately related to her husband and vice versa.

A case may even be made for the unity of well-known couples who became, in their marriages, less than ideal but represented husbands and wives who were committed together to an unknown future: Adam and Eve, Job and his wife, Ahab and Jezebel, Abraham and Sarah, Isaac and Rebekah, Ruth and Boaz, Aquila and Priscilla. Of these couples, one member is not thought of without the other. For good or ill, the twain became one flesh.

When solidarity—and solidarity is the word one chooses for this meaning—enters a marriage, the acts of one become the acts of the other. The occupation or work of one is the occupation or work of the other. Empathy and identity run sufficiently deep that the joys of one appear to be the joys of the other. The pain, even physical suffering, of one becomes the pain of the other.

The sense of blaming each other, or reserving credit for one without attributing equal virtue to the other, is rejected as inappropriate. The burdens and blessings are divided between the parties, reducing the weight of the one and sharing the euphoria of the other.

Even when it is clear that their accomplishments are not evenly divided, the principle of sharing together in all things holds force. This sharing is assumed by the couple and may be discussed at appropriate times. Who knows how much credit belongs to the silent, the less active, the supportive member? He who stays by the baggage shall receive an equal part as the one who goes out to battle. It is a biblical principle which provides insight into any moral or human institution.

As I perceive my life, I could not have completed my goals without my wife's close identification with the process. Over the years I have earned several academic degrees, served in various professional assignments, written a number of books and spoken often in several countries. Why should I not have her name alongside mine in every accomplishment? She knows I remember what she has done. And she shared "in one flesh" my sorrows, my sickness which was almost unto death and my misfortunes. All these, pleasant and unpleasant, were integral to our marriage and intensified our understanding of our unity.

Marriage is a shared experience between a man and woman, perhaps with children. They play and laugh together; they suffer and cling together. They reject the idea that personhood for them is to be understood without each other. If it were otherwise, they would not likely have chosen marriage. They could have legitimately selected the single status. But marriage provided an overlap which, if ideal, welds together at every seam. "The twain shall be one flesh."

FOR DISCUSSION:
1. Do you perceive marriage as substitution for the independent expression of your personhood?
2. What does marriage *solidarity* mean?

QUESTION

37. How will you react to each other's contradictions?

About three months later someone told Judah, "Your daughter-in-law Tamar has been acting like a whore, and now she is pregnant."

Judah ordered, "Take her out and burn her to death."

As she was being taken out, she sent word to her father-in-law: "I am pregnant by the man

> *who owns these things. Look at them and see*
> *whose they are—this seal with its cord and this*
> *walking stick."*
>   *Judah recognized them and said, "She is in*
> *the right. I have failed in my obligation to her—I*
> *should have given her to my son Shelah in*
> *marriage." And Judah never had intercourse*
> *with her again.   (Genesis 38:24-26 GNB)*

Men and women, married or not, are guilty of large and small contradictions in what they say and do. Ambivalence is a characteristic of human nature. Persons wish to be and do, and not be and do at the same time. The problem is compounded by hypocrisy, competition, laziness and self-interest. Although human contradictions are common, persons are offended by them. Mates often handle the consequences of their ambivalence poorly.

Some contradictions include: (1) desire for physical intimacy and resistance to intimacy at the same time; (2) desire to communicate and resistance to communication at the same time; (3) desire to be sociable and resistance to sociability at the same time; (4) desire to work and resistance to labor at the same time; and the like. References to some of these problems appear in other sections of the book.

You may allege that your mate is contradicting himself when in fact he may not be. He may just be inconsistent. Differences between persons in understanding, awareness and perceptions are well-known. When you think differently from your mate, it is easy to feel he is inconsistent in his behavior. His alleged inconsistency offends you, but because he is not aware of any inconsistency, he may react nonchalantly to your objections.

For example, you both may have planned for some time to go shopping. Then at the last minute he may say, "I really don't want to go shopping." "But," you say, "you promised—you don't keep your promises." Instead, you might consider saying, "I'm glad you said that. I don't really want to go, either!" Or you may say, "Okay, dear, but I think I'll go anyway, because there are several things we need." We should not be so rigid that we can't change our minds. The ranges of possibilities in human behavior should make husbands and wives reticent to find offense in shifts in tastes, attitudes and conduct.

It is easy to cite the foibles and idiosyncrasies of others and miss them in ourselves. This seems also to be inconsistency which requires generosity from our mates and friends. But that generosity is hard to come by. The offense is sufficiently irritating that most persons respond in some negative way—silence, protest, argument or anger.

Contradictions in marriage relationships are interpreted by offended mates not as expressions of basic human nature but as evidences of disinterest in or lack of love for one's mate. They are enlarged in confrontations as proof of moral weakness, even outright or deliberate efforts which are sinister and evil. And some contradictions may be just that—sinister—but this question is not concerned with the deliberately pernicious use of contradiction. The concern here is with the common experience of being human, which includes the ability to aggravate through contradictory attitudes and actions.

One of the best solutions to the lack of consistency is acceptance of each other even in contradictory behavior. The problem of ambivalence will arise inevitably. Patient family members need not enlarge the matter by becoming offended and railing against the offender. Humor sometimes (almost always) is helpful in reducing the negative effect. Discussion may resolve despair and tension if the climate at the moment permits objective discussion. Perhaps later, at an opportune hour, the issue may be analyzed profitably.

FOR DISCUSSION:
1. What are your views about common human contradictions?
2. Have you observed any contradictions in your relationship up to this moment?

3. How have you handled contradictions in others, like your parents or friends?
4. How will you treat each other when you "change" your minds on some issue without "reason"?

QUESTION

38. Do you believe in careful, sensitive listening?

Listen before you answer. If you don't, you are being stupid and insulting.
(Proverbs 18:13 GNB)

Verbal communication between family members ought to begin with concentration on listening. The value of effective listening is well-documented. In business seminars, the topic of "active" listening is discussed. And where active listening is done and evaluated, dramatic, positive results appear. Persons listened to are happier in their work (their communications and ideas count for something, raising their sense of self-worth), and problems are more readily solved (input is made by those who know the most about the problems).

Many effective professionals in premarital and marriage counseling not only are sensitive listeners but they virtually compel husband and wife counselees to listen to each other. A counselor, after receiving a volume of material from one person, will often, without other comment, pass the statement to the second counselee, saying, "What is your response to what you have just heard?"

The first experiences of listening may not be happy ones. The person called upon often flounders, asks for a repeat of what has been said, and may be challenged on his subsequent interpretation. At length the counselees begin to listen to each other with care. A new habit may be established in the sessions. And if a facilitator can inspire the two before him to listen to each other, he feels assured of improvement in their situation.

Listening is divided into several types, each appropriate and vital in its place. *Social* listening is important, although it does not appear to be. It is basic to all social intercourse. Contacts between persons, changes taking place during conversation, and leave-taking are generally achieved through common and oft-repeated vocabulary. "Good morning," "Hello," "Excuse me," "Goodbye," are examples. They are heard and responded to. Their use informs listeners they have been seen and acknowledged, which is a way of suggesting the worth of the listeners. A listener's appropriate response returns respect to the first speaker.

This ritual is vital to marriage. Mates should express and respond to social exchanges between them which acknowledge each other. When mates are angry at each other they do not wish to speak to each other, even in a neutral situation. And if exchanges must be made at these times, the nonverbals of voice and body may express disdain. There ought to be effective listening for common friendship even in families.

Listening may be *therapeutic*. The purpose of this type of listening is to heal troubled persons. A crying child, a rebellious youth, a grief-stricken woman or a discouraged man, will likely need listeners who will comfort them, bring them back to an awareness of reality situations. What is said and heard relates to emotional concerns. Perhaps what is said is a cover-up for something hidden deep within the individual. Later the issues related to causing distress may be discussed, but not until comfort and relief from suffering are accomplished. Listening to heal is important in a family. All members ought to learn how to listen sensitively in this sense. Too often therapeutic listening or listening to the inner (sometimes unspoken) message is disregarded. Many persons do not know it exists.

Listening may be *instructive*. It is practiced in order to

learn. It follows both social and therapeutic listening. Having established social contact, assured that no significant emotional barriers will interfere, communicators and listeners proceed to inform one another. Listening to learn ought to be taught and practiced as a means to carry family experience to its happiest conclusion. If learning by listening is understood, the communicator and listener will respect each other, both taking attitudes and using language which focus on processes, facts, conclusions and perceptions.

Listening may be *critical*. That is to say that, at last, a person becomes an evaluative (critical) listener. At the highest level of intellectual exercise a person is called upon to evaluate a situation, a statement or a person. It is difficult to do, sometimes offensive to sensitive persons who presume that all evaluation is negatively critical or fault-finding. Many persons cannot be listened to critically, evaluatively. They cannot bear the emotional experience. But for persons who are open and free, who are confident and sure of their relationships, there is reason to be listened to and to listen in evaluative ways.

The course of family life is improved if all members may open themselves to reviews of personal and family conduct, interests, ideas and assumptions. However, if a member is neither flexible nor open to evaluative processes, the other members will not succeed by pressing the issue. It may require many years of effort for an insightful mate to gain agreement on analysis of family and personal needs through active and effective listening.

FOR DISCUSSION:
1. Do you understand and practice the different types of listening?
2. Do you listen to others in the way that you wish to be listened to?

39. Do you believe in talking over matters and sharing in decision-making for the family?

No more lying, then! Everyone must tell the
truth to his fellow believer, because we are all
members together in the body of Christ. If you
become angry, do not let your anger lead you into
sin, and do not stay angry all day. . . . Do not use
harmful words, but only helpful words, the kind
that build up and provide what is needed, so that
what you say will do good to those who hear
you. . . . Get rid of all bitterness, passion, and
anger. No more shouting or insults, no more
hateful feelings of any sort.
                    (Ephesians 4:25-26, 29, 31 GNB)

There is no real need to talk over inconsequential matters between persons who love and trust each other. Some couples are impractical to the point that every detail of their lives requires discussion at the summit. It is likely in such instances that there is little self-confidence or self-esteem. Trust is difficult for those who lack confidence in themselves. And at the beginning of a marriage the expectation of mates often includes communication about every detail of their lives. Conversation may become pedantic.

Even so, mutual decision-making is good for the family and the individuals who make it up. The individuals are respected, their opinions are valued and they have rights which they can verbalize better than anyone else. When family members talk seriously about their concerns, a protective wisdom emerges which wards off mistakes or reduces their force. The man who refuses to listen to his wife is not only insensitive but is certain to make more judgmental errors than would otherwise have been the case.

After setting a habit of sharing family concerns, members develop respect for their own consensus. When love and honor are integral to a marriage there is also a sincere attempt by each person to understand the view of the other, but not in violation of evidence or reason. This exploration encourages a checking process and delay of decision-making until all members (or nearly all) agree upon the course of action.

The process of talking out issues requiring decision or policy making is highly instructive to children. They learn how to solve problems and how to respect others in the process. They learn to sublimate pride and know-it-all attitudes. No one person knows enough to make all decisions.

Alert persons begin to understand how to talk to family members—the best time in the day, the best voice modulation, the best place in the home or elsewhere. Talking calmly, deliberately, looking at one's partner, responding favorably or gently in doubt to this or that in the other's presentation—all assist in the process. The plentiful use of serious, nonjudgmental questions moves the topic toward conclusion.

Shared decision-making, like many other features discussed under these questions, is not only educational to children, but prepares a mate (likely the wife) to solve problems when death enters the marriage. Many women, bereft, have no practical understanding for managing their affairs when divorced or left as widows.

FOR DISCUSSION:
1. Do you know how to ask questions without offending?
2. Do you believe decision-making belongs to only one member of the family?
3. Do you recognize that shared problem-solving is an educative process helpful to both children and mates?

40. What is your language style?

The man answered, "This woman you put here
with me gave me the fruit, and I ate it."
                                    (Genesis 3:12 GNB)

Happy couples tend to use plural rather than singular pro-
nouns in relating to each other. The situation for Adam and
Eve would have been significantly different if the verse had
reported: "And the man said, We took from the tree, and we
did eat." The guilt of our first parents would have been just
as real, but the solidarity of the couple would have made the
situation more bearable. The "twain is one flesh" is a principle which may and ought to be used in the various kinds of
relationships between a husband and wife—and their children. "That is our house," not "That is my house." "Those
are our children," not "Those are my children." "We make
decisions together," not "I make this decision, and she
makes that one." "We do different things at the same time,"
not "I go my way and she goes hers."

Autocratic persons use autocratic language which falls
upon their listeners like surly commands from a master to a
servant. Husbands are more likely than wives to fall into the
habit of communicating with an air of superiority for several
reasons: (a) influence of parental patterns in formative
years; (b) disrespect for the intelligence of women; (c) belief
that authoritarian language is necessary to establish husband leadership in the family; and (d) expression of emotional problems. These reasons may account for the habit,
but they do not justify it. Women may be autocratic in their
language for similar reasons, amended to express the role
circumstances characterizing women. Language in a marriage should be expressive of equality between husband and
wife.

Profanity or swearing (the terms are currently inter-
changed), which is abusive or vulgar language, is common-

place in general social intercourse. The "four-letter" words are openly used in the language media and have become habit, so commonplace that even some Christians are using them without awareness of their unattractiveness. One of the fallouts of student and other confrontations following 1964 was public adoption of language formerly reserved for private conversations between persons who had no objections to the use of vulgarity. The broader use has permeated communications between mates. General insensitivity by persons using vulgar language creates marital tension among many couples. For many people the use of swear words has become so habitual that they are unaware of their habit or its effect.

Some language is inflammatory. Some writers call inflammatory language "gunpowder words." These are the ones that irritate a mate. Nearly everyone dislikes some words, nicknames or slang. There is no adequate defense for using vocabulary that deliberately offends, although some mates insist on employing it.

Other communication offenses occur when one member is negative in attitudes. He will use disparaging words to diminish persons, concepts or achievements.

Oblique words tend to approach problems with a sideswipe. Innuendo and implications grow out of the discussions and conversation. When issues are not treated straightforwardly, confusion and hurt feelings result.

Jokes that make fun of people are not genuine jokes. Though they may seem to be humorous, they are intended to wound. Humor, when genuine, is one of the most effective tools in building a family. When misdirected, it becomes a means of torture, a form of cruelty.

Repetitious words "rub it in." The emotional irritation of the talker expresses itself in the repetitions of his speech: "I told you.... I told you.... I told you." The listener feels there is no recourse but to respond in the same irritable manner.

Affirmations, pleasantries, smiles and loving gestures introduce happiness, a sense of well-being and love between those who practice them. Why family members snarl at each other, withholding reinforcement for peace and confidence, is a mystery of major proportion.

FOR DISCUSSION:
1. Do you like the words you use with each other?
2. Do you like the voice each of you uses in expressing yourselves?
3. Are you aware of the facial or body expressions each uses in communicating? Do you like what you see?
4. Do you have favorite places where you like to talk?

QUESTION

41. Do you believe in counselors to help you solve personal problems?

> *The way of a fool is right in his own eyes: but he that hearkeneth unto counsel is wise... The advice of a wise man refreshes like water from a mountain spring. Those accepting it become aware of the pitfalls on ahead.*
> *(Proverbs 12:15; 13:14, LB)*

Every person has a right to a physician and a counselor. Both should be sought out as early as a serious need arises in his life. Nearly all standard personal problems are solvable or manageable if the individual maturely confronts his situation early enough.

Following World War II, when there was a dramatic increase in divorce, E. E. Masters of Beloit College studied dozens of marriages which were acknowledged to be unhappy. More than one-third of those studied had consulted marriage counselors in efforts to improve their relationships. None succeeded! Masters rightly concluded that the couples had waited too long to seek help. Problems had been permitted to fester for ten or more years. They were too deep to be extracted and cured.[39] Just as cancer when detected too late destroys a body, some problems not confronted soon enough destroy marriages.

The male ego is often a barrier to solving marriage problems through counseling. More women than men are willing to seek help, although there are significant exceptions to the general pattern. A couple should clearly agree before marriage, and before any storm appears on the horizon, that a counselor may be needed, early or late in a marriage.

Judge J. Earl Lyons, stressed the need for early counseling:

> We need greater understanding and acceptance of what early counseling and casework can do.
>
> So many problems could be solved in the beginning stages if people would realize they are showing wisdom and strength—not weakness—by getting expert help.
>
> I have urged so many troubled persons coming into this courtroom to get professional help from an available agency. . . .
>
> . . . many of them want to believe their problems can't be solved or that there's something shameful in getting outside help. [40]

To believe that one may solve a personal problem without assistance may be as foolish as believing he may solve a major medical problem without a physician. A mate commonly argues, "We can solve our problems ourselves." In a very large number of cases it doesn't work out that way.

However, it is known that many problems do "go away." It is not easy to identify the ones that will dissolve. Two people with generous attitudes, flexibility and spiritual resources may expect to find solutions growing out of their own conversations, personal growth, reading and adjustments. They will sense in most cases whether the problem is one that will go away naturally.

Responsible counselors warn the public against too great

expectations for counseling. Amitai Etzioni, the eminent and forthright sociologist at Columbia University and director of the Center for Policy Research, sounded a needed warning about unwarranted expectations for counseling. After noting that popular columnists often refer their questioners to "professional help," Etzioni pointed out that the professionals may not be as helpful as implied by the columnists. He suggested that therapy may not be appropriate in a number of cases because therapy is weak or helpless in treating some problems. It *will*, of course, be helpful for many people, but we must not put it in the place of a God who can meet our needs.

Counseling, said Etzioni, is more likely going to benefit young persons than the elderly, and more likely to be helpful to counselees who share the subculture of the counselors. A middle class white may not be able to bridge the difference with a ghetto black. A Christian may be offended by a non-Christian, or vice versa.

Some counselors are effective in one kind of therapy, like behavior modification (overcoming addictions), and others use a generalized approach (family problems). And treatment of schizophrenia is more complex than treatment of mild depression, with schizophrenia requiring more skills in a counselor.

Etzioni was concerned about the results that the counselee and counselor wished to achieve: to feel better, to gain understanding, to get a job, to dissolve a habit. He noted that neuroses (anxieties) were easier to treat than psychopathologies (impulsive lack of self-control, absence of guilt and shame). According to Etzioni, depression, sexual dysfunction, and some psychosomatic illnesses are easier to treat and show more success in treatment than do alcoholism, drug addiction, and suicidal tendencies. He argued that persons should never give up even though ". . . it is not wise to bank on psychotherapy being able to solve problems, especially severe ones. . . ." Common problems like "infatuation with a teacher, marital tension and loneliness may be helped by therapy—or the mere passage of time." He stated further: "If there is one rule a person can follow with relative assurance, it is: the more severe the problem, the less likely that therapy will be effective. The less you need it, the better it works.[41]

For young married couples the course of action ought to be clear enough. When aggravations hang on, when they are not weakened or dissolved in a short and reasonable period of time, a counselor is recommended. Problems in marriage for youthful persons are more responsive to solutions, mainly because those problems are not long-lived, and they are confronted by mates who have more flexibility in some matters than they will possess in later years. Sometimes the wisdom of "old age" is better seen in some members of the younger generation than in some who are chronologically old. But the main point here relates to the age of the problem, not the age of the person with the problem.

The assurance for a happy future is greater when a couple concludes, before marriage, that a counselor will be sought as soon as an impasse occurs. With an occasional exception, the counselor should not be a close friend. The couple should not seek an amateur, but someone whose skill in the field is known. In one state ministers who practiced counseling and certified marriage counselors were found to be most effective from among available professionals. They may have encountered troubled persons earlier in the history of problems than the more highly trained psychologists and psychiatrists.

For persons who experience normal problems and opportunities in life, premarital counseling may be the first formal "counseling" experience they have had. It should serve them well, but no matter how excellent and complete before-marriage counseling may be, it is generally insufficient for marriage happiness and solidarity. Within twelve weeks after the wedding ceremony the marriage has begun to shape itself according to changing or reverting attitudes in the bride and groom. Their childhood experiences and their perceptions of their parents emerge from the recesses of their minds and influence their conduct. This is a crucial time for the couple.

Both the husband and wife should return to their premarital counselor for a review of his opinion and file on their premarital sessions. He should ask penetrating questions, and they should openly respond to his queries. This is a good time to sense that counseling does not hurt, that one's ego is not shattered, that our self-image can be wrong and that marriage problems (and most others for that matter) are amenable to problem-solving, if they are confronted early enough and open-mindedly with an empathetic counselor.

Some couples refuse assistance, arguing that marriage counseling is new and untried in the society, that it has become a popular industry only since World War II. Earlier generations received no professional counseling, and their marriage statistics appear to be significantly better than recent ones. The response to that observation is that marriages have always carried deep problems, but our forebears survived their ordeals: (1) with the aid of ministers, doctors, and wise elders in the community, and (2) with final and binding lifetime commitments.

Present society is broadly secularized so that ministers are not included as family problem-solvers as they once were, and marriage commitment is often not binding for life, but transitory. In a society that treats marriage as something that cannot survive unresolved conflicts, even small ones, divorce becomes the solution. If a couple enters marriage determined to stay married, willing to tolerate some conflicts, seeking assistance and applying solutions, the results will be happiness and marital solidarity.

FOR DISCUSSION:
1. Are you prepared to review your first weeks of marriage with your premarital counselor three to six months after marriage?

2. Are you embarrassed at the thought of reviewing your intimate problems with a counselor?
3. Are you willing for your mate to seek counseling if that mate wishes to do so?

42. What are your personal and family goals?

We can make our plans, but the final outcome is in God's hands... We should make plans—counting on God to direct us.
(Proverbs 16:1, 9, LB)

Success is generally related to goal-setting. If one does not set goals, how may he know that he is successful? For success is related to achieving purposes which have been designated in advance. And yet it is surprising to discover not only that most persons do not set goals, but actually criticize the principle of goal-setting. Some Christians are reluctant to project their futures because they believe the Scriptures oppose goal-setting, and they feel that planning for the future robs persons of flexibility and the practice of faith. In point of fact, the opposite is the case. More flexibility and faith occur in projecting one's future than in waiting for the future to happen. When plans are not made and implemented, events become accidental even if they are pleasant and presumed by observers to be successful.

The Scriptures do not contradict the concepts of planning. "Take no thought for the morrow" is an unsatisfactory translation of a passage which actually means, "Do not worry about tomorrow." And one way to avoid worry is to plan.

Goals are not purposes, but are designed out of purposes. If it is my purpose (general) to become a better man, my goals (specifics) are formulated to achieve this purpose. To become a better man, I determine to read a chapter of devotional literature each day.

Goals are measurable. Anyone, by checking the evidence, can state categorically whether his goal has been reached or not. If I decide to save money (purpose), I may set a goal of saving $5.00 a week. This is measurable. Anyone may check my savings book and ascertain if I deposited $5.00 each week for a year. To measure a goal one must set a time frame and provide a record of conduct related to it. The record may be the word of a faithful witness. For example, if I purpose to improve my physical condition I may determine to rise at six o'clock each morning and ride the exercycle for 15 minutes. I do it, and my wife affirms that each morning I arose and did as I determined that I would. The goal was set and reached.

Weekly, monthly and yearly goals are relatively unimportant unless long-range goals are designed to make them meaningful. The *shortest* long-range goal should be about five years ahead. A longer projection is often better. My only moderating concerns in these matters are: (1) my own limitations, and (2) God's will ("If the Lord wills, I will do this or that.")

A couple entering marriage ought to have long-range goals based on time schedules for completing education or developing self-improvement, having children, selecting an area in which to live and working at an occupation. Those goals should emanate from the hearts of the prospective bride and groom and their belief in what God would have them do.

No one—not parents, not friends—can determine the goals for husband and wife. Not even a counselor. But the counselor attempts to help focus the couple's attention until at least a few long-range goals are discussed. Then short-range, perhaps annual, goals are formulated in order to assure progress to the later larger objectives. One of the purposes of a counselor is to show how the goal setting process works and how to keep it working.

Goals may be improperly set because of false information, poor self-evaluation, neglect of appropriate processes or conflict created by competing goals. For example, a couple may decide to have a baby during a year when the wife will be expected to work in order to purchase a home. In this case the arrival of the baby and the home acquisition conflict. One must be delayed.

Goals should be determined by careful preparation, issues discussed with persons holding expertise in related areas of interest, costs calculated, a trial run attempted and the ideas and course of events prayed about.

A couple should be ready to change goals when the circumstances require. Goals are goads, not morals. Goals are not cast in concrete. They are to be used as guides. If a new guide and a better road are found, the old should be abandoned. One of the great problems for goal-setters is that they often insist that a goal must be followed through and kept at all costs. This may be the largest impediment to many persons, the fear that a goal is an inflexible moral commitment. It is not. It is a tool for effective living.

Whether or not they are aware of the fact, most person do set common goals. Every future appointment made on the calendar, every airline ticket purchased for a future day's flight, every purchase of a home, every vacation decision, every application for a job or college, suggest goals and planning. What if these easy, natural gestures were expanded and refined for all of life's future? A bit more projection, some stretching of the imagination, and a belief in making things happen will cause one to set goals.

Setting goals, refining and amending them later, is hard work. Most persons are too lazy to try seriously. And if they do try they feel ignorant and incapable of formulating plans. Even companies which highly tout goal-setting seem fearful of futurism. Not more than one-half to one percent of them set goals for their firms, although they are stern with their salesmen to set personal goals in making calls and writing orders.

A young couple would benefit greatly by implementing

the practice of goal-setting. Both personal and professional goals ought to be designed: (1) Personal goals include spiritual, physical, educational, geographical, family, social and material goals; (2) professional goals include work, company, advancement, earnings. By way of illustration, spiritual goals might include: reading the Bible through in two years, praying 10 minutes daily, attending church twice weekly, including one new family each six months for friendship evangelism or giving a tithe through weekly budgeting. All of these are measurable and include the important time factor.

One of the barriers to goal-setting is that persons may be somewhat effective without goals. In times when workers are rather well paid, when mobility is upward and the general necessities of life are relatively easy to come by, there is resistance to the hard work of designing goals. Goals may not be necessary to survival, but they are necessary for achievement of potential. The world is constructed for the survival of the common man. Goals are for the uncommon. Persons without goals are adrift, and sooner or later they will drift into some port, likely not one they would have chosen. Goals put a rudder on the craft and drive the propeller. There is likely enough energy to move the ship into a desired haven.

At the time of this writing a friend of mine told me the story of a college classmate who designed his courses to obtain the special learning he desired. Following university education he was determined to spend three years working in an office in Washington, D.C., where he would learn how government functioned in the area of his interest. Other goals were set by this student to gain his purpose. He succeeded admirably and early in the course of his life. Success was virtually inevitable for him.

Another young man purposed to get married, make a million dollars, and become governor of Oklahoma. By setting goals to meet his purposes, he made them all. He even became a senator from Oklahoma, and, in 1960, was one of several men considered for nomination to the presidency of the United States.

FOR DISCUSSION:
1. What are some of your large purposes?
2. What are some of the goals that will achieve these purposes?
3. Is it not better to show one's faith by setting goals and rely on God's help in achieving them, than to do whatever casual life inspires and claim it to be God's will?

QUESTION

43. When did you have a physical checkup? What were the results?

My dear friend, I pray that everything may go well with you and that you may be in good health—as I know you are well in spirit.
(3 John 2 GNB)

Among the most common causes for tearing families apart are the "Four D's: desertion, divorce, disease and death." These four enemies, taken together, leave one out of every four children in America fatherless. Desertion and divorce are commonly discussed as marriage issues; disease and death are seldom considered. Certainly, if health were improved, death would be reduced as a harsh factor in growing young families.

Each party to a marriage should feel obligated to seek a complete physical checkup. Even if the results are negative but you decide to get married anyway, the decision was made in light of a knowledge of the facts, rather than ignorance. More married couples have made decisions based on knowledge of physical problems than is commonly believed. Medical histories of one or the other betrothed, sometimes both, may show that the couple should not bear children.

For example, a bride from a family with incidents of hemophilia would likely choose not to generate children. Such a decision is vital for a man as well as a woman and should be a shared experience, decided before marriage.

Mates should be sufficiently interested in each other's health to take care of themselves and encourage sound health practices in their family. To agree on such patterns in advance could reduce possible confrontations later on. Agreements made before you marry are less likely to result in tension than efforts to agree after you're married.

And one needs to know what to advocate. A study made by the University of California at Los Angeles reviewed the habits of 7,000 Californians and showed that the average length of life of persons was extended 11 years if several habits were followed with self-discipline. They included: (1) eating a good breakfast; (2) eating three meals daily on a regular basis; (3) exercising vigorously for a period of time two or three days each week; (4) sleeping seven or eight hours a night; (5) drinking in moderation or not at all; (6) avoiding smoking; and (7) keeping weight down. [42]

In counseling couples, one discovers that most of the best rules for any phase of marriage could be successfully followed if each partner would do his part for the other. For example, if the wife is willing to take on the duty of caring for the nutritional needs of her family (about half of the seven habits listed in the previous paragraph), she nearly assures lengthened life and health for those she loves, including herself. But that means arising in time to prepare breakfast (studies show that millions of American children enter schoolrooms every morning without a breakfast adequate to sustain them until noon). It means also that she will prepare the remaining meals with at least a basic knowledge of nutrition. To succeed she must be creative in preparing a variety of tasty and attractive dishes so that her family will accept a regimen with appreciation, even enthusiasm. In short, someone must care enough for the family to become an informed çook.

Such a caring person will know that juices, cereals and

milk beat sweet rolls for breakfast. Fruits with unsugared cereals, varying the fruits and cereals, make the breakfasts more interesting. That cook resists between-meal snacks for herself or himself and seldom, if ever, offers an unscheduled snack to a family member. If there is one stolen, she lends no support to the culprit. More family cooks should take their jobs seriously to become competent.

Too often they are lulled into false pretensions about their achievements. A few dishes, perhaps starchy, fatty or sweet, are well done and reproduced with some frequency. The family members get used to the fare, even praise the cook for the meals prepared. But why settle for this vicious cycle when a creative approach will add years to your life and life to your years?

There's more the wife and mother can do. By encouraging exercise, by regulating scheduled hours for eating and sleeping and by serving as a role-model in abstinence from sweets, alcohol and tobacco, she sets the example for the healthful habits which lengthen life and cause persons to feel better.

Before marriage a prospective bride should review her expectations and hopes for the health and welfare of her family. If her groom smokes and/or drinks, even in moderation, she should seriously consider if she can accept those habits. Approximately one person in three will increase a drinking habit to the point where he becomes a problem drinker, even an alcoholic.

It commonly takes 10 to 20 years to make an alcoholic, but young drinkers can do it faster. A teenaged drinker is likely on a crash course which will cost him both marriage and occupation before he gains his 30th birthday. Amateur observers, overpowered by romance, are seldom objective in evaluating the future conduct of a loved one. Any person who, at the outset of marriage, accepts in a partner a standard violating his own cannot be totally fair in lodging a protest later, even when the problem deepens in that partner.

More information is becoming available about the deleterious effects of stress. Stress affects nearly all human activity. Collegians discuss stress as a major problem for them. It is believed that among businessmen stress counts for most early heart attacks. Again a wise woman (for women bear the largest family responsibility in domestic areas) will conduct her work to reduce stress, and she will attempt to provide the tranquility that her family requires. On occasions husband and children violate her best intentions, but she will succeed sufficiently often to make the effort worthwhile. Because early marriage is often fraught with stress, which is suspected of influencing the mental and physical health of family members, at least one member of the family should become deeply aware of the importance of the matter and take responsibility for reducing dangers.

FOR DISCUSSION:
1. Do you recognize the importance of the issues of family health?
2. Are you prepared to accept monitoring of family habits? Or will you interpret it as objectionable and nagging?
3. Are your own habits healthful?
4. Are there any differences between you on this issue?
5. If so, how will these differences be resolved?

QUESTION

44. Where do you plan to go to church?

Let us be concerned for one another, to help one another to show love and to do good. Let us not give up the habit of meeting together, as some are doing. Instead, let us encourage one another all the more, since you see that the Day of the Lord is coming nearer.   (Hebrews 10:24-25 GNB)

There is a church in nearly all communities that will accommodate the personality and character of a family. Citizens are usually limited to one country or government. They have a few choices, generally, of schools or points of employment. They may select several clubs or social groups. But there may be as many as 30 or 40 different churches, denominations or fellowships in a community. Some are liberal, some conservative; some formal, some informal; some traditional, some faddish or new; some strict, some casual. There is a church style for every family. No excuse should be made, "I cannot find a church that fits my idea of a church."

Too much evidence is available to prove that spiritual life and church affiliation are beneficial than for someone to deny effectively the worth of a church to a family. The services of a church are free, unless an individual is willing to tax himself (as he should) to support the ministry. The minister serves many functions, from the cradle of a child to the grave of a man. The minister is imperfect, sometimes unavailable, sometimes ineffective in the resolution of a particular family problem, but so is everyone else a failure on occasion. For what he gets and for what he does, the minister is generally several leagues ahead of others who care for and serve people.

The church building serves its purpose. If simplicity is preferred, there are cement block churches or little clapboards a hundred years old. Others rise like silent towers, with great stained glass windows and cavernous rooms. The music, ministry, programs and general services of a church will assist a family, children and parents, to develop solidarity for that family.

Anyone examining the statistics about the positive influence of the church and its ministries upon the family and the individual lives of members will have to acknowledge the value of the church. A Christian counselor generally feels that those who find fault with the church, to the point of avoiding their own involvement, are providing veiled reasons for their own weaknesses. One of those weaknesses may be their ignorance about what the church has done and will do for families and individuals.

Counselors discover that church attendance is a chore in families that are critical of ministers, leaders, programs or other factors in church life. No one person will be satisfied with everything in any church—or any other institution, for that matter. By active participation a person can effect change in his home church for the benefit of his family. Much of the kind of criticism offered by religious persons comes from phlegmatic individuals who tend to leave work and duty to others. To achieve our purposes, to meet the needs of those for whom we are responsible, there ought to be personal involvement in a church community which entails cost in time, effort and money.

FOR DISCUSSION:
1. What kind of church do you wish, as a couple, to be a part of?
2. What denomination is most appealing to you?
3. What contribution, personal and financial, should you make to a church?

45. How will you treat religious differences between you?

> They brought the Box and put it in its place in the Tent that David had set up for it. Then he offered sacrifices and fellowship offerings to the Lord. When he had finished offering the sacrifices, he blessed the people in the name of the Lord Almighty. . . . Afterward, when David went home to greet his family, Michal came out to meet him. "The king of Israel made a big name for himself today!" she said. "He exposed himself like a fool in the sight of the servant girls of his officials." *(2 Samuel 6:17-18, 20 GNB)*

> At a camping place on the way to Egypt, the Lord met Moses and tried to kill him. Then

> *Zipporah, his wife, took a sharp stone, cut off*
> *the foreskin of her son, and touched Moses' feet*
> *with it. Because of the rite of circumcision she*
> *said to Moses, "You are a husband of blood to*
> *me." And so the Lord spared Moses' life.*
> *(Exodus 4:24-26 GNB)*

Michal, wife of David and daughter of Saul, loved formal, liturgical and institutional forms of expression for her faith. David was casual, informal, unstructured, public in his expression. Zipporah, daughter of Jethro and wife of Moses, was reared in a different faith from that of Moses. Her husband, a son of Israelites, was a worshipper of Jehovah, and although he flagged in his devotion for a time, he returned to God and his calling. The shift in direction distressed his wife.

Norman Vincent Peale asked the question: "Is religious difference an important factor in marriage difficulties, and if so, why?" To the query he wrote:

> Indeed it is, and a very important one too. It is too often ignored by young people considering marriage. A West Coast panel of judges, lawyers and pastors lists religious differences among seven major causes of divorce. These causes of marriage breakup, in the order listed, are: (1) money; (2) drunkenness; (3) sexual disinterest; (4) marrying too young; (5) religious difference; (6) jealousy; and (7) the Hollywood love myth.
>
> These authorities state that "a bride's statistical chance of divorce is three times greater than average if she goes to the altar with a different religious background than her husband." While many young people marry in the belief that tolerance is enough, they discover that much more is involved. A different culture pattern, basic differences in thinking and

way of life complicate the problem. Young
people would definitely be wiser to date and
marry within their own religious pattern.
However, mixed marriages, religiously speak-
ing, are not impossible, though certainly more
difficult. [43]

During the lifetime of even a Christian marriage there
will arise differences over numerous religious issues. Christians sometimes split up and end their marriage.

Changing a minister may be as traumatic for a sensitive
person as changing a beloved family doctor or personal
friend. A replacement is confronted with different attitudes
by members of the same family. Children may be supportive
of the new minister, parents may be disenchanted. Tensions
may become so open that the ministry of the church is
undermined.

Different styles develop for family members. Some may
prefer casual programs in which structure is underplayed,
language is pedestrian and congregational participation is
integral to the service. Others prefer liturgy, formal services,
preaching in the great tradition. A couple may be divided on
worship styles. Like David and Michal, husband and wife
may find the differences to be divisive.

Some become involved in missionary and other programs. They give generously. Others wish to be anony-
mous, and the less involvement the better. So a couple must
decide how sacrificial the family will be, what projects will be
supported.

The desire for family worship runs deep for one mate,
and is avoided by the other. Prayer and Scripture are made
subjects for argument rather than means for molding the
Christian family. Advanced planning for personal and devotional exercises will save on disagreements as marriage
experiences evolve. The place of family devotions is a constant cause of tension in some families.

Tensions may rise to create various problems: family
members begin to argue over religious matters, some may

terminate church relationships and some may become judgmental. Christianity, meant to liberate, is turned into cause for faultfinding. Spiritual pride rises. Unhappiness, even disgust, follow.

Each person, even in a family in which there is large responsibility for the members, must leave all other persons to God. One's duty is to live his own life, make his own witness at appropriate times and be an example of his faith.

FOR DISCUSSION:
1. Do you feel that you will be able to leave your mate's spiritual growth to God?
2. What is the likely area of greatest difference between you relative to the Christian faith or personal conduct?
3. What has been your experience up to the present time in making individual judgments about the religious faith of acquaintances?

QUESTION

46. Are you willing to let God change your partner?

The morning after each feast, Job would get up early and offer sacrifices for each of his children in order to purify them. He always did this because he thought that one of them might have sinned by insulting God unintentionally.
(Job 1:5 GNB)

In an address to the 35th Annual Convention of the National Association of Evangelicals, Donn Moomaw stated: "We follow the Word in condemning divorce and disintegration of the home, while at the same time our homes reek with abusive legalism and dehumanizing lovelessness. We often trivialize the Word by making it relate to relatively safe issues but are negligent in following the Word in the areas of ethics and social practice."

The ease with which some persons, especially in the family, play God with other persons is not easy to explain. Perhaps human and spiritual pride is great enough that men and women feel they should appoint themselves judges over those near to them. Love, liberty, generosity ought to be in sufficient supply and be respected so that each person grants to every other the privileges and rights he believes belong to him.

When persons live together, as they do in a family, there is a tendency to become judgmental, to impose one's conscience on each other. This is observed in children who watch for infractions in their brothers and sisters. Their perceptions and responses are not so much directed toward correcting errors as to gain moral advantage, to see the others punished. There is a kind of greediness in them. When these attitudes appear in adults, they seem uglier than in children.

One of the most common areas for judgmentalism is past record. Sins, errors, poor decisions, bad habits (even when recovery has taken place), may be draped on a husband or wife for years. No change or forgiveness is permitted. The judgmental partner does not see himself as weak, but is keenly aware of the weaknesses of others, especially members of the family.

Each member is called upon to love the others in the family, to accept them, to live a model life himself and to let others determine their own way of thinking, feeling, acting. This does not mean that all actions, even if sincere, are good or of the same quality. Many are wrong, some are evil, but unless the acts are illegal, God must be the judge of persons and their actions. Yet man is commissioned by God to make laws and judge those who break them.

In premarital and marital counseling sessions one prospective mate was offended that the other was unwilling to condemn the use of tobacco as a rank sin (neither smoked or expected to do so); one mate lost respect and affection for her husband when he refused to tithe (although he was a Christian, the husband failed to apply fully biblical insights); another could not accept the political party of the other (many Christians believe that devotion to a party or political philosophy is devotion to their country, and these are spiritualized); a woman became persuaded her husband did not love her because he liked dogs and raised them (she was not frightened by dogs, but disliked any distraction in her husband from her own interests); another doubted her husband's love because he would not give up a habit (a habit she countenanced during the engagement period); and another doubted because her husband would not attend church with her (he had attended only spasmodically during their courting days).

We may suppose that it would be well to go to church, to give up debilitating habits, to tithe, to agree on issues important to each person, but it is also true that husband and wife may be in love, sense marriage solidarity, and not be alike, feel alike or act alike. At times a couple, in acceptance of differences, accent love, even beauty, in marriage by the manner in which differences are managed.

One of the most uncomfortable characteristics observed in any Christian, either in marriage or social intercourse, is the "playing God" attitude. This attitude causes persons to become judges when they were meant to be witnesses. Spiritual life and integrity in at least one spouse are efficient builders of a marriage relationship, but spiritual pride is a fast and efficient destroyer of it.

FOR DISCUSSION:
1. Are you willing to leave the moral judgments of your loved ones to God?
2. Are you a person who thinks, especially on some issues, that you are always right?
3. Are you aware that the same Holy Spirit guiding you may be guiding your mate, even when perceptions differ between you?

47. Do you understand the husband's leadership in the family?

Submit yourselves to one another because of your reverence for Christ.

Wives, submit yourselves to your husbands as to the Lord. For a husband has authority over his wife just as Christ has authority over the church; and Christ is himself the Savior of the church, his body. And so wives must submit themselves completely to their husbands just as the church submits itself to Christ.

Husbands, love your wives just as Christ loved the church and gave his life for it.

(Ephesians 5:21-25 GNB)

Many Christian men confuse leadership with domination. Through autocratic attitudes, disguised as headship duties, they compel obedience from their wives and children. If they can get away with it, they carry the pattern over to other relationships, including those with church members and fellow workers. Assuming male superiority based on an interpretation of Scripture—that any man is the leader of any woman—they become dictators. And even if their dictatorship is basically benevolent, it is nevertheless objectionable to many responsible and democratically-minded persons today.

The meaning of marriage roles in Scripture is related to husband and wife, not to man and woman. The submissive attitude referred to in Ephesians 5:22ff. has to do with husbands and wives, not with all men and all women. To employ the submissive role of wives referred to in Ephesians 5:22 to all men distorts the meaning of both the passage and marriage. The previous verse (verse 21) refers to submission of both husbands to wives and wives to husbands. In context the verse suggests that all Christians are to be submissive to one another.

The often quoted 22nd verse personalizes the matter for wives. Marriage, symbolized in Christ and the church, is the issue discussed. And it is appropriate to argue that the passage deals with the doctrine of the church as the doctrine is analogous to marriage.

If leadership means what it appears to mean in the Scriptures, it is assigned to a person by those who determine to follow him and acknowledge him. In a truly free situation no one becomes my leader unless I grant him that privilege and responsibility. He can become a dictator without my support, but he cannot be my leader without it. A father, mother, child or some other member of the family may become its leader. That person earns the right to leadership, partly by the things he or she does and the wisdom he or she has, but as much as anything else, because other family members grant leadership.

In Christian marriage, primary family leadership presumably rests upon the husband-father. He becomes the leader if he expects to fulfill his role as the Christ-figure in the family. His responsibility in the matter should be to work aggressively on himself to become Christlike. As a person strong in his spiritual development, he becomes worthy of serving as leader, and almost without thinking about what is happening, family members defer to his leadership.

Wife and children are instructed by the Scriptures to accept their roles and assist other members in carrying out their assigned responsibilities. For example, children are commanded to the role of obedience to their parents, and the parents are called upon to exert fair discipline to assist their children in carrying out expectations. If the children acquiesce they are promised "long life"—the first commandment *with promise*—that is to say, the first contract between God and man.

The big issue, which some feel to be unjust, concerns submission of wives having more talent than their husbands. Many wives are wiser, more articulate, more energetic, perhaps more of just about anything than their husbands. If they function in biblical patterns they will likely provide assistance to their husbands to learn and practice leadership. They will become gracious to assist, even educate him, in whatever way possible to accomplish his assigned role. If he refuses to accept his privileged duty, she will do whatever she must to assure the future of her family. She will provide whatever he omits, after herculean efforts to help him have failed.

Why bother? Why trouble oneself to work through the husband-father? (At one time I seriously doubted that a wife should be concerned about a dolt of a husband. She should get on as fast and efficiently as possible without waiting for a laggard, or, as is common, one who is docile and pleased to have her take charge.) Years of counseling have convinced me that husband-father leadership in Christian marriage is worth every effort. It helps each family member and the situations he finds himself in.

Father leadership, when available, is best for the children during their important formative years. Mother has them for the preschool period, then they begin to look to father as their model and protector during the formative school years. Mother generally gets them back after they reach early maturity, but there is the stamp of their father in them. Daughters commonly seek husbands like their fathers, as sons seek wives like their mothers.

A woman may survive with honor whether she is dependent or independent. A man may not. He is generally held in derision if he is perceived to be little more than a drone in the home—or "second" to his wife, the mother of the children. Even women who prefer to take charge look with disdain on "weak" men.

Husband-father leadership, rightfully practiced, is best for the marriage. Someone has to be the "senior partner." Generally the husband has the equipment for it—the voice, the physical size, the schedule of life. But even in homes where everything is shared in chores, career, or whatever, the wife is presumed to be the manager of the house. (Exceptions to these in life, and other statements to the contrary, do not deny the massive pattern of domestic life.)

Someone will have to be the head of a family to confront attacks on the children by the bullies in the community, to sign his name to an agreement, to sacrifice himself for the family members in a showdown. A wife-mother begins her unique venture with the births of her children. Their needs are more a part of her than they are of the father. He has his duty and he should bear it. He does not take time out for childbearing, nursing or mothering. We need to acknowledge that there are differences between family members and to make them responsible for tasks that take these differences into account.

The husband's headship and fathering make him the natural figure for ultimate responsibility. The perception is widely supported. Law enforcement agencies, sociologists, and others deplore the loss of father-husband leadership in the home. Where it has disappeared, the plight of children, the distress of wives, the increase in problems of social control are well known. Walter Miller's statement is illustrative of repeated writings on the importance of a father figure in the home:

> One of the most popular explanations for the existence of youth gangs is the "product-of-broken-homes" theory. While most scholars regard this explanation as overly simple, they do see the gang and the family as closely related. Youth gangs are in fact more numerous, better established, and more likely to engage in serious crime in those neighborhoods with a high proportion of one-parent families, particularly those without fathers. Some students feel that old gangs in communities of this type serve in part to make up for the absence of a father figure at home. With their stress on toughness and masculinity, the gangs may be helping—for better or worse—to instill the male identity in their fatherless members. [44]

A democratic society elects a president or prime minister upon whom leadership status is placed by the people. He is, hopefully, a leader to match his status. He is not superior to the citizens, but chief among equals. Unless he is stupid (in which case he will be replaced in due time), he will consider the ideas of those he leads. His purpose is to *serve*. The family, in microcosm, is a democratic society led by the husband-father as chief among equals.

FOR DISCUSSION:
1. Are you, as a husband, willing to become all you ought to be in order to lead your family?
2. Are you willing to lead as Christ led his disciples?
3. Are you, as a wife, willing to assist your husband to become the leader he ought to become?
4. Are you willing to be led by him?

QUESTION

48. Do you see each other as equal before God?

So there is no difference between Jews and Gentiles, between slaves and free men, between men and women; you are all one in union with Christ Jesus.   (Galatians 3:28 GNB)

In our life in the Lord . . . woman is not independent of man, nor is man independent of woman.   (1 Corinthians 11:11 GNB)

Man and woman are and ought to be equal, as implied in Genesis 5:2: "He called *their* name Adam." Male and female constitute the race of man. The beginning relationship seems to have been ideal. But the fall of man introduced numerous social problems. Tensions, competition, misunderstandings arose, setting the stage for domestic warfare. Men came to do the hunting and fighting and women came to be preoccupied with childbearing and domestic activities, but such inequities were never meant to be. As a result of these inequities, however, the male has for much of history dominated the female. Care for children prevented women from resisting this domination through the centuries until modern technology gave them the opportunity and time to broaden their interests.

The concept of female subjugation gained some reinforcement from biblical interpretations (or misinterpretations, in the view of many exegetes). Sex roles were distorted with a wife often subjugated in the name of submissiveness. But the Apostle Paul argued that even this imposed difference of dominance and subservience was destroyed in the Gospel. As there is not a slave and slaveholder, or a Jew and Gentile, before God, there is neither male nor female in point of eminence or value. In Christ all are one. That truth imposes considerable responsibility on both men and women to confront their equality and utilize it for family and spiritual benefit.

The key is to so live, so teach, so believe that the equality of all emerges from theory to practice. To keep a man (slave) in subjugation is contrary to the purpose of the cross. All who believe have been set free. The holding of a slave is contrary to spiritual emancipation. To make Jews better than Gentiles, or Gentiles better than Jews, is to defy the work of Christ. Persons are to be understood in their relationship to God more than to each other. To subordinate women is to do the same thing—to nullify the cross of Christ. Christians should believe in and work for rights and justice for all—male and female.

What better place to begin emancipation than in marriage? The wife is equal to the husband, the husband to the wife. They should recognize that equality, and conduct themselves accordingly. God so loved the male that he gave the male a mate. He would not create an inferior being, part human, part beast. One flesh can only be made by equals, who procreate equals, to share equally.

That sharing includes opinions, plans, time, status, hopes, money, children, worship, heaven, liberty, pain, rights, justice, love, empathy, generosity, home, work, personhood, respect, nurture, mutuality, communication, happiness, approval, esteem, sex, virtue, education, health, discipline, forgiveness, ambition, weakness, and many other factors that make up life for all persons.

FOR DISCUSSION:
1. Does the prospective groom fully recognize the human equality of his bride-to-be, with all the meaning *that* truth entails?
2. Does the bride-to-be recognize her equality with her prospective groom, with all the responsibility *that* truth entails?
3. What is the difference between role assignment and equality?
4. What do the various Scripture verses referred to in the introductions to the questions in this book accomplish in your understanding of your role as a husband? As a wife?

49. Do your parents and friends favor this marriage?

Laban and Bethuel answered, "Since this matter comes from the Lord, it is not for us to make a decision. Here is Rebecca; take her and go. Let her become the wife of your master's son, as the Lord himself has said. . . ."
They answered, "Let's call the girl and find out what she has to say." So they called Rebecca and asked, "Do you want to go with this man?"
"Yes," she answered.
(Genesis 24:50-51, 57-58 GNB)

Discussed under a previous question was the fact that one marries not only a mate but a family. The families of one or both mates may be disregarded, even rejected by the couple. The loss is more serious for the couple than for the disappointed families. Newlyweds who have a cordial relationship with their parents, even grandparents, possess a great treasure. They should do whatever is reasonable to maintain and nurture those relationships.

If you become isolated from parents and relations, you become an island cut off from help and comfort. You also rob future children of their right to the love of grandparents and knowledge of family history. It is a serious and perilous business to try to cut family roots and launch a marriage without any concern for blood lines. Orphans, even those ideally treated by foster parents, often seek desperately to find their natural mothers and fathers. They are looking for their roots.

Certainly, some parents are harsh, lack understanding or are unfair and selfish. In rebellion children may sever ties, or in opposition to their children parents reject them. The loss in these instances is tragic, perhaps beyond the understanding of anyone involved.

We are assuming, of course, that families of a prospective bride and groom are intact and are willing to adopt a normal relationship with the newlyweds. Where death or divorce has split families and ended the chance for traditional child-parent-grandparent relationships, there is significant loss. Sometimes substitute grandparents may be found.

Families are products of ancestral and historical backgrounds, as seen in widely different cultures, habits, attitudes, expectations, rituals, and man/woman relationships. For example, South American parent/child, girl/boy and husband/wife relationships are significantly different from their North American counterparts. Even legal problems for an individual in South America may be judged in the courts on the basis of family support of the defendant. If a family is unwilling to argue for one of its members, that member must be "guilty" and deserves some kind of punishment. The marriage of a couple in many of these countries includes family members in important roles for aiding and defending the bride and groom. But in the pluralistic societies of the English-speaking world, families are often left out, even disregarded.

What is intolerable in one family background is, on occasion, virtuous in another. In some subcultures women expect to be physically dominated by their husbands. I have heard of wives praising their husbands for spanking them because they "talked back," or ridiculed them before their friends. Not all women (or men) would tolerate so violent a physical demonstration of displeasure. One couple sought counsel—a couple on the verge of separation—because of a single quick slap which, although sincerely repented of, was not forgiven. In this case, the wife overreacted to her husband's temporary loss of control.

Many marriages suffer in their later years because the couple downgrades the importance of family ties. They forget that persons are born and bred in a family, which in fact marks them with a special identity. To deny that identity leaves a vacuum. They must be reminded that parents are greater blessings than threats to marriages.

It is well to look ahead to the future. Will I be happy with the response of my own adult children to me at the time of their marriages if they feel as I now do toward my parents? Fair is fair. It is the future which is to be lived. That which is past may be used to curse or bless that which is yet to be.

FOR DISCUSSION:
1. What may be done if parents are not enthusiastic about the proposed marriage?
2. What concessions may be made to parents who deny permission or request delay for the marriage?
3. What should be done if parents are divorced and unwilling to participate in the ceremony in any way?
4. What are the young couple's duties to each other's parents?
5. What effort has been made by each party to learn the biographical history of the other?

50. Have you made all the arrangements for the wedding?

Let us rejoice and be glad; let us praise the Lord's greatness! For the time has come for the wedding of the Lamb, and his bride has prepared herself for it. She has been given clean shining linen to wear. (The linen is the good deeds of God's people.)

Then the angel said to me, "Write this: Happy are those who have been invited to the wedding feast of the Lamb. . . ."

And I saw the Holy City, the new Jerusalem, coming down out of heaven from God, prepared and ready, like a bride dressed to meet her husband.   (Revelation 19:7-9a; 21:2 GNB)

A traditional marriage, including family members and friends, has a better chance of survival than the fast, easy, unplanned ceremony. Persons married in church, in a Christian ceremony, with minister and family joining prayer and challenge with the couple, have significantly longer-lived marriages than those who disregard religious amenities and meaning.

The personally-designed wedding ceremony may lose something valuable. The vows, reconstructed to fit the modern idiom, often leave out anything that smacks of differences between the sexes, obedience of one to the other, the possibility and acceptance of such tragic occurrences as illness and death, or the permanence of cleaving throughout life. By omitting the deeper expressions of love, the new vows sometimes seem superficial. The current fad is to create a sense of casualness. Romantic thoughts, bits and pieces of love poetry sound impressive, but the words of selfless commitment are missing. "As long as ye both shall live," has become, "As long as ye both shall love." People are not perfect enough to love *all* the time. But God says they are duty bound. A life commitment will carry them over the loveless periods in their marriage.

The bride and groom should ask themselves, "Given fifty years, what shall I recall from our ceremony? What will life have required of us? What did the mystique of the ceremony do to help us during trying years?"

Weddings need not be expensive or lavish. Some weddings include costly banquets, livery, clothing, personnel and rentals. The honeymoon alone may cost several thousand dollars. During recent years many brides have opted for more modest appointments. Today's traditional ceremony seems more genuine than the ornate social occasions which were the dream of so many debutantes during the first half of the 20th century.

Competent counselors and guidebooks are readily available to assist a couple in planning and conducting a wedding ceremony. The easiest and least costly way is to counsel with a minister and follow his advice. He will suggest what is appropriate in the church he serves, including practice of the ceremony, where to meet, how to approach the altar, what to do with flowers, when the music is to be played, how the bride's wishes are to be respected and the like. He is a friendly lieutenant to have for the occasion itself, resolving conflicts between mother, grandmother and daughter, even between bride and groom, if those potential conflicts materialize.

A minister feels a special relationship to the bride and generally will try to do whatever she wishes to have done. He reassures the bride and groom that despite all the tension they will be married and on their way before the evening is over. They must be patient with family emotions. Even with their periodic piques and tomfoolery, friends wish greatest happiness for the couple.

If a marriage ceremony is to be planned by a professional, the couple should follow her counsel. She will seek information, especially from the bride, and include it in her plans. Some brides put confidence in the florist who, if fully professional, will be helpful in arranging the physical appointments of the wedding. If requested, the florist sometimes monitors the order of the wedding march.

The honeymoon is often disastrous, and couples ought to know and expect that possibility. The intimacy, weariness, the emotional tension, the overactivity caused by the trip itself, could create problems from which the marriage will never recover. Some women have admitted in counseling sessions, "I knew on the honeymoon that we did not love each other. We were not going to be compatible." They were unprepared for honeymoon problems and overreacted to their experiences.

Many, if not most, couples are not compatible on their honeymoon. They would have been wiser to take a long weekend together, return home on Monday, follow routine, and plan a honeymoon ten weeks after the ceremony. (I have no confidence this suggestion will gain a favorable hearing.)

The main point to be made is that before marriage a couple should resist the tendency to keep late nights, follow rounds of parties, and whatever else that is exhausting. Exhausted persons are not themselves, and they do not perceive others in the best light. As they approach their wedding, a man and woman should schedule conversation and prayer, parents and family, planning and counseling, relaxation and intimate discovery. Single life is about to give way to corporate life. It is the end of one and the beginning of the other. The transaction deserves all the attention that a young couple can give it.

FOR DISCUSSION:

1. Does everyone understand that the wedding tradition-ally belongs to the bride, with rights of final decision?
2. Have all arrangements been made, with a checklist sys-tem, for the wedding ceremony?
3. Have all appropriate details been discussed with the min-ister who is to solemnize the ceremony?
4. Have all expenses been approved by the person assum-ing the costs of the wedding?
5. Do all features of the wedding honor God, the Giver of the gift of marriage?

Conclusion

The words which relate intensely to marriage should be thoroughly defined and discussed by each prospective bride and groom. They are:

Mutuality:
The greater the number of shared interests or adaptations to interests, the greater the opportunity for happiness.

Money:
The greater the commitment to advanced planning and debt-free living, the greater the opportunity for avoiding tension.

Nurture:
The greater the similarity between principles and conduct, the greater the opportunity that all family members will develop integrity and grow spiritually.

Love:
The greater the attempt of one member to outdo the other in expressing *agapé* love, the greater will be the rise and fulfilment of lasting romance in the marriage.

Sexuality:
The greater the dedication of one to meet the intimate needs of the other, the greater will be the genuine discovery of each other.

Communication:
The greater the willingness of each to express himself in all matters and listen to the other, the greater will be the understanding of both.

Goals:
The greater the refinement of planning for life purposes, the greater the chance for gaining what the family wants and needs.

Children:
The greater the understanding of the rightful place of children, and respect for their persons and needs, the greater will be parental success with them.

Discipline:
The greater the application of self-discipline and follow-through of all appropriate discipline, the greater the opportunity for a happily ordered household.

Christianity:
The greater the place that God holds in the hearts of individuals in the family, the greater is the awareness of the sanctity and eternal character of the family.

NOTES

1. *Cleveland Plain Dealer,* May 15, 1975.
2. *U.S. News & World Report,* December 8, 1975, p. 68.
3. *Christianity Today,* January 31, 1975.
4. *San Francisco Chronicle,* December 5, 1975, p. 4.
5. See Robert R. Bell, *Marriage and Family Interaction.*
6. See Vance Packard, *The Pyramid Climbers.*
7. Letter to the author in response to his paper presented to the 1975 Continental Congress on the Family.
8. Another letter on the same occasion.
9. *The Spokesman-Review Sunday Magazine,* November 9, 1969, p. 9.
10. Letter to the author in response to his paper presented to the 1975 Continental Congress on the Family.
11. Philip Roth, *My Life as a Man* (NY: Holt Rinehart, 1974).
12. *The Oregonian,* November 13, 1975.
13. *Covenant Companion,* June 1, 1975, p. 29.
14. *The Spokesman-Review,* November 9, 1969, p. 7.
15. Mark Lee, "The Church and the Unmarried," in *It's O.K. To Be Single,* ed. Gary R. Collins (Waco, Texas: Word Books), p. 53.
16. *San Francisco Chronicle,* March 13, 1976, p. 29.
17. Paul Tournier, *The Adventure of Living,* pp. 131-132.
18. Patrick McGrady, "A Lifestyle to Avoid Aging," *Woman's Day,* April 5, 1977, p. 184.
19. *Ibid.,* p. 185.
20. Barbara Cady, Review of *The Dance-Away Lover and Other Roles We Play in Love, Sex and Marriage,* by D. Goldstine et al, *Los Angeles Times,* July 10, 1977, p. 13.